Vague Direction

*A 12,000 mile bicycle ride, and
the meaning of life.*

DAVE GILL

VAGUE DIRECTION

Published by SteepMedia, 2015 - SteepMedia.com

"Vague Direction:
A 12,000 mile bicycle ride,
and the meaning of life."

ISBN-13: 978-1511848060
ISBN-10: 1511848065

Excerpts from: "Bat Out Of Hell" from Epic Records. Performed by Meat Loaf. Written by Jim Steinman. 1979.

And, "Ithaka" from C.P. Cavafy. Translated by Edmund Keeley and Philip Sherrard. 1992.

Cover design by MountainCreative.co.uk

Typeset by Blush Book Design
www.blushbookdesign.co.uk

Copy and editorial assistance by John Mitchell

Some names and locatio
for ethical and editorial pur

For high-quality photog
vaguedirection.com/galler

Please support indepe
naughty stuff like reprodu
permission. Thanks, you r

Find Vague D

vag
faceboo
@
youtube.

Contents

Dedicated to my family, for being there. (And also, because if you don't dedicate your first book to your family, they might disown you.)

Foreword

"IF YOU'RE WRITING A FOREWORD, CONGRATULATIONS! Generally, it's because you've accomplished something, you are already published, and your name is well known." So starts the advice I found for how to write one of these things on the internet. Jump ahead to my name. Heard of me? Didn't think so. I'm not published either. That's two out of the three check-listed qualifications already gone. The third... have I accomplished something? Yeah, I thought I might have in my time on this earth. Then Dave Gill came along and blew my conception of what an 'accomplishment' was right out of the water.

Twelve thousand miles is one heck of a long way. I do that in my van in 18 months. Dave did it in a bit over a year... on a bike. This book is about that journey. It's also about so much more than that journey, dragging us into the heart of what a 'journey' actually is; what it actually means.

I've known Dave for coming on ten years now. Everyone has a mate called 'Dave' and he is mine. We met through a friend I studied with and travelled off to Spain to rock climb before ditching our lives back home in the UK and driving around the West coast of America in a dilapidated, graffiti covered van we affectionately named 'Duchess'. You might have seen us? Two things struck me about him on this trip; the first such extended period of time we had spent together.

Firstly, he's rubbish with money. He never has any.

Secondly, he has an insatiable desire to experience and learn about life, but not in the 'normal' way. Living in the back of a van with two other blokes is testament to that. This desire, coupled with an undeniable talent for filmmaking and photography, ultimately led Dave to this journey and this book.

I defy anyone not to have profound and life-altering experiences when cycling solo around North America - I get freaked out biking to the shops. The long stretches of monotonous pedalling down desert highways; the worry and accumulating stress of not knowing where you'll sleep or what you'll eat; not knowing if where you'll sleep will make you what a bear will eat (solves the previous problem at least); dealing with strangers not knowing if they'll turn out to be friends or if they'll threaten to kill you. These are only a pinch of the considerations that make up the narrative of this ride.

I guess this is ultimately the story of loneliness conquered, and understanding found. Of strange places and strange people. Of not being defined by a stereotype because of your society or culture. Of the discovery that the people Dave met were amongst the most inspiring and amazing people you could ever wish to meet, but that they are not unique in that. There's hundreds, thousands, millions of other people he could have crossed paths with who would have been equally as amazing and inspiring. This book, then, is an affirmation of the goodness of humans.

I hope you get something out of Dave's story. You're a stone if you don't frankly.

Lt. G. Foster RA,
British Army, and writer at Fellicionado.com

Prologue

THERE'S A POOL OF BLOOD IN MY RIGHT EYEBALL. A BLOOD vessel has burst, turning it into a dirty micro-glacier with rivers of red running throughout.

Stress.

I shout out "Fuck this!" and hope no housemates are in the kitchen, because you can hear everything from the kitchen.

Medically, they say that "stress isn't a recognised cause of subconjunctival haemorrhage." Clearly the doctors are wrong, or it's the mother of all coincidences that the only time this has ever happened to my eyeball is now.

I look up at the ceiling, beyond the white paint, focusing on nothing in particular, and have a vivid realisation that this is not working. Sometimes it takes looking at yourself after a while of living in a self-created hole to realise you are not in a good place.

This is the reason why getting a bike and fleeing seemed like the best option.

Don't get me wrong, the stress that acted as catalyst for this story didn't come about through severe hardship. I wasn't like Eminem and didn't live on the streets or anything like that. Although sometimes, when my housemate Chris was around, that was appealing. Jesus, Chris, 4AM isn't the time to start playing your homemade techno music.

No, this story begins as a burned out director in a struggling company. There was probably no need to pack up and leave. But when you're in the hole, you lose perspective, and in that regard I was blind.

Thankfully, it all led to an experience that I wouldn't change for a second.

The story of what happened next is this book.

1

Leaving

SOMETHING THAT TERRIFIES ME IS WAKING UP ONE DAY, having a moment of realisation, and then telling myself: "You plodded through. You spent so much time doing things that weren't worth it that you wasted it, and now it's too late." So it's good to catch the great discontent early, as maybe then there's a chance to do something about it.

I'd reached the tipping point and it had become time to act.

This wasn't just an escape, although it was certainly that. It was also an opportunity to learn from people who had dealt with these same questions and doubts about life, too.

The drive from my flat to our company studio in Manchester felt like the longest commute of my life. All fifteen minutes of it.

The entire weekend had been nervously spent considering how to tell my business partners the news that I wanted out - out of the hole that we'd found ourselves in that wasn't enjoyable anymore. My fuse had burnt up, entirely fizzled out. And to make things sour, I was in business with my brother Neil and friend James. So it was more sensitive than simply cutting and leaving.

When you've invested time, energy, money and what feels like everything you've got into building a company, or anything for that matter, it inevitably becomes hard to step away. And there's that well-known saying - 'never go into business with your friends or family'. That probably originated from a conversation like this.

Leaving would cause a domino-effect, there was no doubt about that. All of our stress was at an all-time high and one person leaving, whoever snapped first, would bring the company crashing down.

We sat. I took out my phone. Looking at the script I'd written over the weekend felt more comfortable than looking up at their reactions. So it wasn't a very courageous or manly delivery. Letting go was news that hurt. Of course it did. There was sadness. There was a brutal release of tension all-round. There was disappointment. But I don't think it was particularly shocking.

I'd spent the last 6 months looking out of the window over the city skyline, thinking about what to do. Something far away, miles away from the exhaustion and the hustle. You can't go for long without believing in what you're doing.

Quitting the company marked the end of a chapter that, at it's height, was packed with incredible moments. But it was time to move on, time for new experiences. Maybe getting lost and embracing something totally new, with only a vague plan, would lead to good things, and perhaps even insights to those unknowns that had been weighing on my mind.

Made more clear after quitting work, part of the desire to go on a big journey was because I could clearly see my 'cards' had lined up. "It will never be easier than it is right now," I thought. And the reason why, was that I no longer had a job to go to, and I was single, renting a room. There were few ties.

I used to love riding bicycles and couldn't recall any bad memories when cruising around on two wheels. So a mission formed in my mind around this concept. A big bike ride. Clear and simple. Why the hell not?

One evening, I pulled up Google Maps, and zoomed out.

The world is so small now and, if we conveniently ignore our carbon footprints for a second, going to the other side of the planet to make good on a silly idea is totally feasible.

Where to go? The cursor moved across continents. The US and Canada shone out as the place.

At first that seemed like a boring option. "It's just like Britain but bigger," people might say. "How unoriginal." And those are thoughts that ran through my head. Part of me wanted to just set off and see where I got to in Europe, but I kept clicking back to North America.

In Europe, my language skills are limited to pointing and ordering un croissant s'il vous plait in a very loud Northern voice, whereas in America I'd be able to have conversations with people, unlike in Latvia or The Antarctic or Comoros. And on this journey, that would be important. That was what the journey was intended to be about.

New York in November was the start. That left 6 weeks to prepare.

At the top of the list was getting a bike. I didn't know anything about cycling a long way. By searching online, it was clear the bike of choice, by a gravelly country mile, was a 'Surly Long Haul Trucker' and would cost about £1200. Nope, sorry. Not got the budget for that.

There wasn't much budget at all to be honest. I'd been trying to save from work but that silly Surly price was the cost of several months of travel time. So I sacked off all advice from people far wiser, and went on eBay armed with £150.

Being 6'5" can be on the cusp of 'awkwardly tall', and this was no exception. The only used bike that was the right size was a 'Trek 7.5FX', and as luck would have it, the seller was based half an hour's drive away. Fate? Maybe.

"I rode from Newcastle to Scarborough on it once," the seller, Gary, said proudly. "The chain snapped a couple of times, but I reckon you'll be okay." He was very confident that this steed was bomb-proof, and his confidence made me confident.

"Looks great," I said without hesitation, handing over some notes.

With a bit of TLC and some small additions, it seemed up to the job. A bike is, after all, just a metal frame with two wheels. That blasé attitude would get me into trouble a lot over the next twelve months. "You get what you pay for," they say. They're right.

With the bike sorted, next came the task of getting rid of everything. Combined with meagre savings, selling stuff was a vital piece of the puzzle, and it was a lesson in forced minimalism and radical simplification.

There's a lot of stuff we probably all have that we can live without. So I sold it all. Every last thing. The car, camera gear, computers, surf boards, anything that wouldn't be carried by panniers. It was liberating, like feeling the wind on your balls after stepping onto a naked cruise. Eradicating stuff leads to an eradication of stress. No more blood-filled eyeballs after this.

The planned route took a while to figure out. It made sense to follow the seasons to avoid any of the super-harsh winters. No one likes too much ice. So with a starting point of The Big Apple, I aimed to cyle South, straight down the coast to Florida. From there, 'The Southern Tier' - a popular cross-country route - would take me from Florida to California, taking in all the Southern states. Then, I'd aim to follow the Pacific coast North to Alaska.

At this point, the map looked like a huge U-shape. A loop was never intended, but the U-shape looked empty, lonely. An obvious challenge, then, was closing the loop. So a final leg, one that involved riding back across Canada and dropping down to finish back in New York again, seemed like it could provide some kind of meta-closure. Maybe after riding a loop, life would make more sense. Or maybe not. I had no idea.

From the earliest seeds of this journey's concept, I wanted it to revolve around meeting a bunch of people and chatting to them about life.

The physical bike journey was intended to be just one part - a way of getting between some interesting characters spread across the continent and getting a bit healthier in the process. The second part was about learning from people, about talking to them about the lessons they'd picked up just by living. Riding a loop which took in 19 US States and 6 Canadian provinces ought to provide plenty of opportunity for both.

During the final few weeks in the UK, planning got hectic, and I didn't ride the bike at all. This went on and on - no riding whatsoever - until after a while the avoidance became intentional. I'd packed the bike and had seen what a full set of pannier bags looked like. Lifting it, with everything on it, it was outrageously heavy. There was no damn way I was going on a "training ride."

I was intimidated. Going on a ride before 'the ride' would make me realise that the whole thing was a terrible idea. There'd be plenty of time to get in the swing of things when the journey actually began, and being on a new continent separated by the Atlantic would remove the incentive to turn back.

Departure day. I was excited, a little anxious too. My family knew about the burnout, and they were supportive, if a little worried - they could see that I was out of my depth but didn't plan on coming back until it was done.

In New York, there was snow. A lot of it. The Nor'Easter storm had hit the east coast about 6 hours before landing, bringing with it freezing temperatures and heaps of the white stuff. It was exactly what that coast didn't need. Storm Sandy had torn through just a couple of weeks beforehand, which had destroyed a lot of the East coast, so it was a bad run of luck.

Upon seeing the snow, The Fear arrived. This trip had me completely and utterly out of my depth. My mind shifted from fear to anticipation to excitement. This was it, and the only thing left to do was to get on with it. I didn't have any idea what was going to happen in the coming days, weeks, months, year. That was thrilling.

2

A New Beginning

RIDING OUT OF NEW YORK CITY WAS AN INSTANT SHOCK TO the system.

Everything would probably become much simpler from George Washington Bridge, but getting there, and navigating out of the busiest city in the US in the process, had to come first.

That morning was really the first taste of naivety which would stick around for a long time. A Magellan GPS was mounted to my handlebars. I typed in 'George Washington Bridge', and went wherever it told me. Which was a mistake.

Following the computer was quite successful for the first half of the day. From Queens, I cycled through suburban streets, away from any particularly major or scary roads.

There were still heaps of snow on the sidewalks, but fresh snowfall had stopped, plus it had taken a couple of days to get organised before setting off riding, during which time the city had kicked into snow-mode and sent out the gritters. Americans don't have a heart-attack when it snows unlike British people.

The bike was perfect. This was going to be a total doddle, easy, no problem at all. As far as first days went, you couldn't ask for more.

That luck wouldn't last long. An hour or two passed. The roads became much busier. I weaved in between yellow cabs and bumper to bumper traffic, only occasionally thinking 'hmmm, something might not be right here.' Even approaching the tunnel, I didn't clock that this might not be the right approach. It was the NYPD's sirens and the officers shouts that confirmed that, yes, going through the dark, unlit bridge on a bicycle was illegal.

"What the hell are you doing? Can you not read?" The officer was angry. "Didn't you see all the signs? You can't ride a bicycle through the tunnel. You'll die."

With hindsight, he had a valid point. So with a warning and new directions, I eventually found the bike path that follows the Hudson River up to the George Washington Bridge. And as a side note, there is a gaping, enormous difference in stress levels when you compare riding on a cycle path to playing slalom with NYC's traffic.

George Washington Bridge. A marker, a symbol. Lots of things would become 'markers', but this one represented starting, because it was the exit from the city into something more mysterious. So there was really only one thing to do. I delved into my bag, and fished out the camera to record the moment.

On the bridge is a path, away from any traffic, it's a clear run. It's a relatively long bridge, so you're on it for a while, and there's walkers as well as cyclists, rollerbladers, and all sorts of other people using the path.

Perhaps it was obvious to some onlookers that this was the start of something bigger than a day ride, because as I filmed the crossing, steering with one hand and holding the camera in the other, a rollerblader called out from behind.

"Safe travels, man!"

On turning around to spot who it was, and to shout "thanks!" in reply, that's when I crashed into the side of the cycle path and fell to the floor, tearing a hole in my trousers, cutting my knee, bending the bikes derailleur and only just managing to stop the camera smashing into the concrete. Day one. It had been a matter of hours, and wasn't the most glamorous of starts.

But you've got to iron out the niggles early on, right?

The next few days were, physically, a massive shock to the system. Firstly, I was using a Brooks leather saddle which hadn't been broken in and notoriously takes a couple of weeks of excruciating riding to become comfortable. Secondly, with a no training approach, setting off was the first time my legs and back muscles had been used so intensively. Thirdly, the first few days didn't involve much decent sleep at all.

Those aspects combined had me very quickly asking myself 'What on earth am I doing?'

The loose, unorganised approach to navigation over those first few days didn't help either. In my mind, there were really only 4 sections of the journey. The first was to Florida. The second was to California. The third was to Alaska. And the fourth was back to New York. In between those points, there weren't many specific plans.

The GPS was set to 'St Augustine, Florida' and was providing the navigational heavy lifting. This casual, unattached approach actually led to some fantastic impromptu experiences over the next year, but on riding through Union City and Jersey City on day one, a Saturday night, I vowed there and then to take navigation a little more seriously. Because it would suck to get murdered straight away.

I posted a blog about the first day on the road, and a reader called Rob posted a comment.

"Cycling through NE New Jersey!" he said. "And in November! And in the dark! No offense, but 'where angels fear to tread' comes to mind."

Maybe that summed up why I'd been feeling on edge.

Bizarrely, it was quite a deflating end to the first day on the road, in a way. Leaving the city with enthusiastic gusto, I thought I was ready to take on America, to live an adventurous year, to get by in a minimal way, to always sleep in a tent and catch fish with homemade spears. But riding through these first New Jersey cities had been so intimidating that all thoughts of wilderness went out of the window and I found the nearest motel in the city of Linden to escape the nerves until the following day.

Day one over, and I still felt very underprepared.

3

The First Glimpse

JUST SHAKE OFF THE NERVES. BRUSH THE INTIMIDATION TO one side.

With every pedal stroke and every mile, I began to get further away from the built up urban environment, and further away from a feeling of being utterly uncomfortable.

The transition was quick. It only took a few hours for The Fear to become less significant. The dense urban sprawl turned to scenic towns, and my mind was dragged along with it, turning from being nervous to being upbeat and much more calm.

I pedalled fast. It was cold, autumnal, the snow had gone, and the tree lined roads were now bathed in deep oranges and reds, blanketed by fallen leaves. Hopefully the first day had just been a hiccup. Just ironing out those niggles, remember?

After 63 miles, the light began to fade. There were some woods to the side of the road in a town called Burlington. It was secluded, discreet, and the branchy floor was soft. It was the perfect place to camp, to learn the routine that would soon become familiar, and to get into the swing of things.

Consistently camping for a long period of time can be an experience of contrasts, depending on your mood. In the more wild areas you find quiet, nature, isolation. That's what people are drawn to. It's why people love camping. Bliss, an escape, relaxing. But when you're tired or sick and on the move, sometimes those same factors can quickly become the bane of your existence. I was yet to learn it, but camping on this journey would turn into a fluctuating and temperamental way of life. The best times were nights like the one in Burlington, when it all went well.

To quickly explain, 'stealth camping' is a term that has been adopted by bicycle tourists. It means to camp somewhere subtly, without being seen and leaving no trace, and also at no cost. It's the number one key to enabling people without Richard Branson's bank account to sustain long-term travel. As it really doesn't take many nights in motels or even on campsites to result in very scary monthly outgoings and rapidly dwindling budgets. On this journey, it would be necessary to put on a cheapskate hat and happily wear it.

Slowly packing up and moving on, I hadn't learned how to leave with speed in the morning yet. But I was refreshed from the first night of camping, and becoming happier and happier with the routine.

A keen cyclist called Isaac had sent an email a few days earlier, suggesting that we should all grab some dinner if we were in the same place and if the timing worked, and the timing did work, so this evening was when Isaac, Sarah, and I had arranged to meet.

Isaac and Sarah were husband and wife, living in Cherry Hill, New Jersey. Both of them were into cycling, which was a little off-putting, because even though I was apparently a bicycle traveller now, not enough time had passed to feel anything like one.

In the evening, a big pickup truck entered the concrete strip mall parking lot and the driver honked, waved and drove towards the obvious fully loaded bicycle that rested against a wall. Isaac climbed out. Dressed in a green polo shirt, tall and with a shaved head, he'd finished work for the day as an R&D chef at Campbell's Soup HQ. We made our introductions, shook hands, high fived. There'd been a few funny looks over the course of the first couple of days, and Isaac was the first person I'd met who 'got it'. He understood the appeal of a journey like this and was encouraging about the whole thing.

We went to meet Sarah at their apartment. She was around 5'5", and very smiley. Once we'd made our introductions, we went for dinner at The Cheesecake Factory. I couldn't understand why we were going to a factory that made cheesecake, but they assured me it was only a name, and they suggested that, going forward, eating a lot of calories would be important to stay positive, upbeat, and energetic over such a long time.

We ate, we laughed. It was great to have a proper conversation with two positive people. Isaac admitted how he constantly dreamt of going on a big bicycle journey, just packing up and doing it, but he'd found himself caught up in Corporate America, and was now in a system which was hard to step away from.

But as he spoke, as he talked about what he'd do were it not for the job, there was an ambitious flame in his eye. You could see that deep down was an idea that revolved around freedom. He'd read everything he could about it, he knew about the routes he'd take, the gear he'd use, the things he'd do. With such an underlying motivation, it was difficult to believe that he would put off implementing his dream plan for long.

Now full and waddling, we headed back to their apartment. There were several bikes lining the walls, and we spoke about why cycling had become such a big part of their lives.

For Isaac, it had really grown to become an important part of his routine and lifestyle.

"Cycling for me, on the weekdays," he said, "provides a clear mind when I go to work. I commute about 4.15 in the morning time, and nobody's on the roads. I see a few bikers, and it's peaceful. I get to work, and I'm calm. I don't need coffee. I don't need anything to wake me up. I'm happy... On the way home, it's a decompression. I think a lot, and it unwinds me, so when I get home I'm pretty calm, ready to go chill out..."

And for Sarah, it was the all about health.

"Exercise is just something that I miss from when I was in college," she said, "when I used to walk everywhere. It's a nice way to build that into my structure, because you don't get that much in America, so why not build exercise into your day?"

It was getting late. It seemed rude to stay much longer. Sarah and I spoke about possible areas to stealth camp, and it seemed like there were probably some decent and secluded spots nearby.

After a quick shower, I began packing up to leave. But whilst the hot water had been falling, in the living room Isaac had been calling someone. They both looked at me with a smile.

"Hey man," Isaac grinned, "I travel a lot with work and have a bunch of points saved up. Sarah and I spoke about it earlier and we just got you a suite at a hotel in town. Oh, and I asked them if you could have an extended lie-in and they said yes, so you can just chill out, get a late start and start tomorrow super relaxed."

This totally blew me away. Was there a catch? I pinched myself at how kind two people who I'd literally just met could be.

This was something that would happen a lot over the next year, but here it was brand new. It was the first glimpse I'd had into people's overwhelming, raw generosity. Turns out, there's a lot of it out there.

4

On The List

IN THE FIRST FEW WEEKS, LIFE ON THE ROAD IS ONE OF mostly highs. You pedal all day, you naturally detox, you experience 'the zone' - a place when your thoughts are clear and all worries vanish. Every sunset that you pedal into inspires you with the knowledge that this is the start of something. It's all just one massive positive cliche, really.

Sometimes those positive thoughts were diminished, when witnessing the recent effects of Mother Nature, whilst riding on the coastal roads of the Atlantic. The destruction from Storm Sandy had literally torn homes and businesses apart. Many towns were deserted. They would have been quiet anyway, as the places on the coast were largely seasonal and it was November, but this was a different type of quiet. Roofs missing. Windows boarded up. For some, Sandy had royally fucked them.

Heading South, I pedalled right down the coast. It seemed likely that during the cross-country sections of the trip, the ocean would quickly become missed. To me, a sea breeze and rolling waves encourage a healthy mindset and I'm most relaxed around the water, so whenever possible I tried not to take the proximity for granted.

It took a few days to get to Cape May, which is at the very Southern tip of New Jersey. When the land runs out, you get on a ferry which drops you off at Lewes, in Delaware. To continue South means riding down the Delmarva peninsula. It's a clever name encompassing three states - Delaware, Maryland and Virginia. And from the small town of Lewes at the top of the peninsula, the land becomes thinner and thinner, until it runs out again in Eastern Virginia.

State lines became a marker of headway and a mood changer, over time. And on the peninsula, they passed by fast. The simple signs bring with them a realisation that momentum is underway, and sometimes sadness when you realise you won't be back for a long time, if ever, if that state has been particularly special.

On the peninsula, the landscape bounced between open coastal roads that passed empty crab shacks, to natural evergreen forest tunnels that were so dense they didn't pass anything at all. It was easy to find a state of flow in the tree-lined natural tunnels, whilst the wind rustled down them like a funnel.

This was really the spot where I cut my teeth, too, when it came to learning the whole living-on-a-bike routine. A quiet place to learn the ropes. Most Delmarva nights seemed so quiet that camping was relaxing. There weren't many people around, so it was possible to camp on football fields, in fire stations, on grassy tops that overlooked the water. Anywhere, really. That freedom is bliss compared to some places where it was necessary to be more strategic.

It took four days of cycling down Delmarva to reach the most Southern town on the peninsula, Cape Charles, a small town of around 1,100 residents, separated from the mainland by Chesapeake Bay.

At 11PM, as I arrived into town after a night ride, the main beach was lit up with the flickery glow of the overhead streetlights. It was a Friday, and fitting with the theme of other towns on the peninsula, it was eerily quiet. You could look across the bay and see the blurry and distant lights of the heavily urbanised Virginia Beach and Norfolk cities, knowing that it wasn't quiet over there. After the intensity of leaving New York, I was still relieved to have come down the peninsula, a route away from the crowds.

The wind on the beach was cold and strong. Turning the GPS on revealed a park nearby, 5 minutes ride away. The grassy bank that was perfect for stealth camping overlooked a river, and rows of trees protected this spot from being visible from the road. Leaving the tent in the panniers, I unpacked the sleeping bag and bivy bag, and lay down, falling into deep sleep instantly. Sleep is incredibly easy to find when you live on a bicycle. You're always knackered, you can sleep anywhere, anytime.

6.15AM came, and the alarm on my phone buzzed.

'Urghh, stop, stop now.'

Try as I may, attempting to convert into a morning person was not working, and I turned off the alarm and went back to sleep, rising later.

Back at the beach, there was a lady in the distance, walking close to the water, constantly picking things up from the sand. Driftwood and rocks and bottles and the miscellaneous stuff that has a way of ending up on the shoreline.

An hour later we met, on a street set just off the beach.

She was Dora Sullivan, and she turned out to be the mayor of the town. She was originally from Egypt but had been living in Cape Charles for 15 years, and was wearing bright yellow glasses and a permasmile. We chatted outside her shop, Sullivan's.

All the stuff she'd been collecting would end up like the items on display. Quirky art made out of driftwood. Sea-worn bottle hangers. Visual art created with influence from the water, the sand and the salty air. Dora had an infectiously optimistic zest for life that would make anyone with a soul grin.

She saw the bike, the gear and the dark pockets of sleep that were hanging under my eyes, and as a mayor would when talking about her town, she was curious.

"Where did you sleep last night?"

There are times when you have to be careful about the answer to this question. Do you tell the mayor that you slept by the side of a river instead of contributing to the local economy and finding proper accommodation in the town?

"Erm, on the grass by the river in the park. I arrived late," I admitted.

"Don't worry, I won't tell anyone." She laughed. "And I'm the mayor! But you must be so tired! I can tell - just look at your eyes! You look so tired. But I bet you didn't have any problems did you? There's zero crime in this town. Seriously. Zero! None!"

She was proud of the town, which I guess is probably the one asset that makes someone a good candidate for mayor.

"Come inside," she smiled, "I've got Oreos and a Coke with your name on it. Just leave your bike outside. I'm dead serious, there's no crime here! None! Don't even worry about it. Don't lock it up, there's no need. You could leave it here for a decade and it would be right where you left it when you got back."

We went inside to a back room of her shop. Behind the immediate facade of a retail store was the control centre of the town. Corridors and a conference room where she did mayor-y things around a large wooden meeting table. It reminded me of a spy film, where you pull a book on a bookshelf in the right way, and a whole new world of secret intelligence is revealed behind the walls.

I'd never met a mayor before, and wanted to know what her role actually meant. As she explained, she spoke in such an upbeat tone that we quickly found the conversation drifting from mayor topics, to what she thinks is most important in living a happy life.

"I think the thing that people miss is the fact that it's not so much about what you do every day," she said. "It's your circle of friends. It's family. And then you've gotta dream. It's so good to dream... I make things. I look like a bag lady. I go to the beach and pick up driftwood, rocks, glass, fishing lures. I found half an ore the other day. And then I make something. It's therapy, it's the thrill of the hunt and the smell of the sea."

We spoke about how to approach being lost in life, how to find your calling.

"Have a list," Dora beamed. "A list of the things you want or need to do. At some point, you're going to have to do one of those dreams. You're going to have to do something on that list, or you'll catch yourself in your own lie because you didn't do it."

It only took a few minutes, maybe even just seconds, of being around Dora for her optimism to permeate. And I realised that this journey was just a version of doing something on that list.

Fired

JUST OUTSIDE CAPE CHARLES IS CHESAPEAKE BAY BRIDGE. It is massive, at 4.3 miles long. When it opened in 1952, it was officially the worlds longest continuous over-water steel structure. The bridge is the only way of getting from the Eastern Shore of Virginia, to the more urban Western Shore on the mainland.

As a major tolled transportation route, it's generally always busy, with thousands of vehicles passing through every day. The bridge revolves around motor vehicles, there's no cycle lane or path or anything like that running parallel to the road, and bikes and pedestrians are banned from using the bridge.

I began riding from Cape Charles, to the bridge toll station, arriving at the toll plaza at 11AM, with no idea about the bridge or how to get across. The bridge officials saw a lone cyclist queuing with the cars and waved me forward, where they explained about their policy, and said to wait for half an hour or so until a bike shuttle would be provided.

Jermaine Daniels arrived in his white pickup truck. He was a former Union worker who now worked part-time at the Bridge. He was dressed in his official, reflective orange and yellow jacket, and was in his sixties.

We teamed up and grabbed the frame of the bike to lift it into the back of Jermaine's truck, before starting the drive across the bridge, to the mainland.

That drive was an honest, no holds barred one. In contrast to Dora the previous day, Jermaine didn't seem as fired up on life and beaming positivity, but he certainly told it how it is and had valuable things to express. It was immediately obvious how this guy was switched on, smart, and insistent. In every word he spoke, there was a powerful flame that burned bright. A powerful flame that was sick of getting treated badly by the Virginia corporations.

Jermaine spoke about his beliefs, and about working culture in Virginia.

"When you're on the bottom of the pile, it's important to understand that shit rolls downhill," he said with a seriousness. "And you catch hell trying to shovel it back up. Virginia is a right-to-work state, but we refer to it as a right-to-work-for-less state, because of how it reduces the worker to a subservient status of having no say in the workplace."

"And also, being at the will of the employer. So, if the employer comes in one day and says 'alright, everybody's wearing pink socks tomorrow', well, if you don't come in with pink socks on, your ass is fired, and there's no recourse. You're fired. You can bitch all you want, but it's legal. Not fair, but it's legal. The idea in America is, as long as it's legal, to hell with it being fair. It doesn't have to be fair, as long as it's legal. We have so many challenges that would make your head spin, man."

During the drive, in between explaining about the state of work, Jermaine burst out with, "Oh man you've gotta see this!" and with excitement, we pulled over onto a pier located on the bridge, in the middle of the bay.

We spent ten minutes walking down the long wooden structure, out to sea, chatting about Jermaine's intense frustrations with the system, and observing the fishermen who were braving the strong winds. He was proud of Virginia, but was angered by it's flaws, like a Londoner talking about congestion.

I filmed some of the chat. It's easy when you pull out a camera for a person to hold back or portray someone who is not the real them, who is scared about saying too much, but Jermaine wasn't like that at all. He was the real deal, courteous and warm and not scared to have an opinion.

What I didn't realise at the time, was that the point he had just made, about shit rolling downhill, would reappear later.

More than just being the longest over-water structure, the Bridge is also known as 'one of the scariest bridges in the world' because of regular high winds, low guard rails, it's height, and lack of hard shoulder.

"Sometimes on the big swell days," Jermaine laughed loudly, "fish can get thrown on the road!"

The short time I spent with Jermaine is a really fond memory. Straight after, I was excited to write a blog post and upload a snippet of Jermaine's video interview, to display his authenticity and beliefs. So a few days later, I uploaded a quick clip to YouTube, without thinking too much about it. It was just a quick, rough snippet video, no big deal.

60 days later, Jermaine got in touch. By that point, I was in Texas and had been going for a couple of months, had met a lot of people, and the specifics of the day had gone from the forefront of my mind. He sent me an online message that was quite to the point.

"Dave this is Jermaine Daniels, the driver that took you across the Chesapeake Bay Bridge. You posted some of our video on YouTube and the bridge tunnel management is ready to fire me even though I said nothing negative about the bridge tunnel at all. It is, as I said, the guy at the bottom catches what rolls down on him. I need to talk to you if you are willing. It would be a tremendous help to me. Call me. I have an idea."

Fuck. A casual video, and now Jermaine was about to get fired. That was the first time I realised how the internet, and it's limitless reach, can negatively effect an individual.

The bridge management had spotted the video on YouTube. They argued that Jermaine was in his work uniform and was therefore representing the Bridge at the time, and that he'd "used derogatory terms which didn't represent the views of the Bridge."

They were going to fire him for speaking his mind. Shit does roll downhill.

I called Jermaine, apprehensive because I thought he'd be fuming and angry with me. Most people would've been. But of course he wasn't. This was Jermaine Daniels. A guy who wasn't afraid to speak his mind about 'the man' but did so in a very calm and collected way and was pleasant to anyone he spoke to. He said that he'd enjoyed watching the video, and recognised there's value in showing a balance.

Honestly, the only thing that was going through my mind was 'Screw balance, what can I do to make sure this guy doesn't get fired?' There might not be a choice in the matter of course, but my aim coming off the call with Jermaine was to have an actionable plan about how to rectify the situation and make sure he didn't lose his job.

I explained that after his message, the video had been taken down, to which he didn't seem to care much. He just wanted to explain what his grand idea was. If this incident resulted in him getting fired, he wanted to produce an exposé documentary about corporate America and the guys at the bottom of the pile. Hopefully we could rectify the situation without a firing.

Eventually we decided that I should call up Chesapeake Bay Bridge's Chief of Police, to explain what had happened. When the Chief answered, he said he was appreciative of the call, although that was hard to decipher through the anger and aggressiveness on the phone. I tried to explain how Jermaine had been a credit to the Bridge that day. We finished the call and the Chief said he would consider everything. His tone had been impossible to read. I crossed my fingers and hoped for good news.

The eventual news was positive. "Thanks for your efforts," Jermaine wrote, "however, management was truly offended by my "opinions stated to a customer". A day's suspension is what it amounted to. At this time I will remain calm about it. However, I stated that I still remain passionate but will contain my self in future dealings with customers."

It wouldn't have been cool, at all, if a video had led to Jermaine losing his livelihood. I vowed to be more careful.

6

Close Call

THE PICKUP TRUCK WAS INCHES AWAY WHEN IT STARTED skidding. The impact would be bloody and fatal.

Learning by experience, or by totally messing up and putting your life on the line, is a guaranteed way to accelerate your learning. As long as you don't die, what not to repeat ever again becomes clear and it forces you to change your ways as a direct consequence.

It was a dark and cloudy December night. A Saturday. Drops of rain lingered but hadn't begun their full leash yet.

That morning I'd woken in the garden of a Fire Station near Wilmington, North Carolina. The Fire Station staff had offered their space, and knowing that it was permitted meant a night free of worry or stress.

There's a lot to pick up about the way of life on the road over the first few weeks. It's immersion learning. Just over a fortnight into it, and post George Washington Bridge incident, I'd fallen off the bike twice. Both times had been a little physically painful, and more just painfully embarrassing.

Once involved attempting to take a photograph, forgetting to twist and unclip my shoes from the pedals, and falling into a deep ditch on a quiet road. No-one saw, which made me realise that, yes, if a tree falls in the forest and no-one is around to hear it, it absolutely does make a sound. Take that, philosophical thought experiment.

The other incident involved pulling in to a Burger King to hijack the WiFi, forgetting to unclip yet again, and falling onto the concrete parking lot, separated, by a thin glass window, from a group of children looking out from the inside. They all saw and found it hilarious, and I tried to pretend it was intentional and then pedalled off.

Both of those times happened in places where falling off was not potentially life threatening. That wasn't the case now the pickup truck was moments away.

The road, the Ocean Highway 17, was one that was constantly busy and always fast moving. There was no hard shoulder but there was a thin strip, a foot wide, which was the only part of the surface which wasn't the actual car lane. To ride along that strip was precarious. It would've been in the daylight too, but it's risk factor was multiplied once the sun went down. It was a game of balance. 6 inches to the left of the tyre was the road, the fast paced cars, the danger. 6 inches to the right, was a small drop as the tarmac ran out, and a grassy, muddy section. One side muddy, the other bloody.

As I rode along this strip, the focus it took to not mess up, and to maintain balance, was intense. Pedal stroke after pedal stroke with eyes focused directly downwards over the front wheel. All whispers of peripheral vision vanished as tunnel vision took over. The cars, trucks, tractors rushed past every few seconds and were almost instantly out of sight, driving into the dark night ahead.

My main bike light was on. The rear flashing light too. But the road formed a dip, and so cars couldn't see over the brow. I was riding in a blind spot. The high visibility jacket barely ever got used. It was buried deep in a pannier bag somewhere, and even though it should've been on, at this particular point on the road, it would've made no difference.

The intense balancing act quickly failed, when my rear tyre got too close to the edge of the tarmac. It slipped into the grass and the mud without any notice. As an unconscious reaction, I swerved aggressively to stop falling.

The reaction spun me directly into the road, and I tried but failed to unclip my right foot in the process.

I was in the road, in the middle of the car lane, in the blind spot. The shoe came undone. I put my foot down onto the surface to pivot and push immediately onto the grass. To get off the damn road.

As I turned and pushed, the pick up truck headlights hit the frame. The beam lit up everything that was even partially reflective. Maybe the jacket would've been a good idea.

The sound of skidding and screeching took over the night sky.

I made one huge push in a last ditch effort, and didn't dare look round. The sound seemed too close, too loud. I thought that this was it. Death by pickup. Half a second, a quarter of a second, not long now until it would hit. Oh shit.

'Push off that leg again. To the grass, just get to the grass.'

The front wheel touched the edge of the tarmac to meet the green blades. Only the rear wheel was sticking out into the road now. A microsecond more of survival and I'd be out of harms way, ready to laugh it off.

The rush of the pick up truck was like nothing else. It was so close, like a tornado passing a hairs width away from an eardrum. But that's what it did, it passed. It didn't hit, there was no impact. I was on the grass and it hadn't hit.

The truck continued to skid and screech. It stopped up ahead. The red tail lights were an intense reminder of the danger that just was.

I was in shock, shaking, out of breath.

After a few seconds, the tail light of the truck turned off. Maybe the driver realised he was static, now sat in the sketchy blind spot as well. The truck accelerated, and did what the other vehicles did - vanished into the night.

In that single moment I vowed to not be so ignorant, and swore at myself, vocally shouting into the night, "You fucking idiot! You fucking idiot!"

In the future I was going to learn from this and do things differently.

Stepping off the bike and beginning to push it to the next town, I was so shaky that the thought of getting back on the bike didn't even register until the following day. Walking as far away from the road as possible, I continued to verbally kick myself.

In terms of overall probability, if you spend a lot of time being near high-speed traffic, the chances are you'll be part of a dangerous incident. Maybe there's a metaphor in there some-where about making sure the risk is worth it.

7

Cannons And
Urine

F AST FOOD CHAINS BECOME A BIT OF A COMFORT-BASE ON A
long solo trip.

Firstly, there's a lot of them in the USA. Secondly, those big
yellow M's that you can see from a mile or more away have internet so, when you want them to be, they are a place to check into
normality for a while. And lastly, you might not expect it, but
there can be a lot of serendipity in the air within those greasy
walls.

I'd arrived the night before in a town called Richmond Hill,
Georgia and camped in the large gardens of Bethel Baptist
Church. In the morning it became clear that I'd pitched the tent
on an ants nest, as my shoes and pannier bags, and everything

else that was kept outside the tent, was crawling with ants. It wasn't pleasant and it was itchy.

Sometimes you get a feeling about how the rest of the day will play out during those first few minutes of waking up. Maybe it's fate. If a day starts badly, it's probably going to go badly until it ends. When it starts well, you're potentially in for a great day. Or so you tell yourself.

Things didn't bode well today, there were ants, lots of them. But something unusual happened under the gaze of a fast food sign.

Two guys walked in. In their sixties. Hawaiian shirts. With them came an immediate atmosphere of fun, which is nice when you've just spent half an hour swearing at ants. Ty and Frank were beaming with smiles and laughing like children. They were excited about something and that made everyone in their presence excited about everything. They sat down next to me.

"What are you guys so excited about then?" I asked.

"Ah! He's a Brit. 'Ello guvnor. How's Queen Elizabeth? London Town awash with raindrops, is it?" Ty was high on life. "We're in town for a civil war reenactment up at Fort McAllister. Reenacting The Battle Of Fort McAllister. Our whole family has come down, my son, grandkids, everyone we know."

You can't drop an event like that into conversation and not get a curious response.

"That's where you guys dress up and shoot cannons and stuff?"

They explained that, yes, they do dress up and shoot cannons and musket's, but it's not a game or anything like LARP (Live Action Role Play), which is where a lot of people get together and pretend to be wizards and live in magical worlds hitting each other with foam swords. This was instead, based around real history. And in this case it was a recreation of an American Civil War battle that took place on December 13th, 1864, when Major General William T. Sherman's Union forces overwhelmed a small number of Confederate soldiers to take the strategic Fort McAllister.

Ty and Frank were intrigued about the bike outside the window, and as was a regular response, the conversation ended in a look of 'why the hell would anyone want to do that?'

"Oh you've gotta come with us to the Fort," Ty proclaimed. "See what it's all about. It's going to be a great day."

You should always accept an invitation to a civil war reenactment.

They left to set up camp. There was going to be a congregation of dedicated civil war reenactors camping out tonight on the grounds of the Fort in traditional 7ft high A-frame canvas tents.

I cycled up a few hours later, just before the battle reenactment began. The grounds of the Fort were magnificent. Amongst the trees, Fort management has done well to keep everything maintained so there's plenty of just-as-it-would-have-been buildings, underground bunkers and trenches.

Expecting a lot of marching people, plenty of noise, and perhaps a little mayhem, for a while I was quite miffed.

There must have been around 60 - 70 reenactors, and far from being an epic battle, there was just a lot of people in period costumes taking a nap in the trenches, muskets by their side. It was quite an odd experience, and I wondered if the soldiers in the actual civil war were quite as sleepy. They probably did grab sleep whenever possible, so maybe this was actually very realistic. Still, sleeping actors didn't drum up the same vivid energy as the thought of an epic gunpowder battle.

At first it wasn't particularly thrilling and it didn't seem like there was much going on, but then I realised there was a whole other side to it. The day was planned, and was playing out in the same way the 1864 battle did. The trees were filled with more people, who weren't asleep.

The Confederate forces who were defending the Fort didn't see the Union lot coming until the last moment. They were literally overwhelmed, and this was reflected in the many reenactors hanging out in the trees.

Speaking to them, it was obvious that this wasn't just a bit of fun, but it was a way of life and their main interest. There were all sorts of people reenacting a variety of roles, from cobblers and blacksmiths under hidden shelters, to cooks and maids in the houses spread throughout the grounds. Everyone was smiling and there was an obvious and strong bond between the reenactors, no matter the age or background.

Already tight communities can be awkward and uninviting for an individual who's not part of the gang. Sometimes people are apprehensive to welcome you in to their group. This didn't happen with the reenactors.

The real battle started. The muskets started being fired.

Everyone woke up from their previous snoozing and started moving through the trenches, crouching down and occasionally peaking over the grassy crest to look for any approaching troops. Teams started marching and preparing for the climactic part of the battle when the Union soldiers would take over. The spectators were asked to move back. They didn't want anyone too close to the cannons and explosions.

A roaring boom. The cannons went off. Marching troops, alive now, not asleep. Soldiers laying down, trying to hide. For a moment it all seemed quite real. There were bangs, booms, whistles from all around. And then, quickly, the battle was won. The Union soldiers took it.

Ty was sat in the woods, around a smoldering BBQ with a few of the older reenactors. The battle had worn them out, so they'd retired to drink home-brew.

He called over, and the group spoke about how they had ended up here.

"I started because my son was introduced to another reenactor in his classroom when he was 13 years old," Ty reminisced, "and he wanted to do reenacting. Well, he was too young because you need to be 16 before you can carry a rifle, but due to the fact that he was about 6ft tall at the time, we sort of fudged it and got away with it!"

"It makes me feel like I'm worth something," a chap called Lawson admitted, "that I was here to do something that happened a long time ago and I can show my children and my grandchildren and other people what it was like. I'm generally a happy person. I enjoy life. I try not to get too down, because life's too short to get too down. I try to stay positive all the time, try to stay happy, and this is something that I really enjoy doing. This is my thing."

All of the remaining reenactors began to congregate around the hub of open fires in the tent area. The white canvas tents added to the realism and a sense that this could easily be 1864.

When the gathering around the fires began to settle down, there were a few people who weren't ready to call it a night. A group of 6 people, including Ty's son Jason, were going to drive to Savannah, to an Irish bar, in their full period costumes.

"Wanna come, guvnor?" Jason shouted.

Yes. Absolutely yes. A pint and a group of people in period costumes. That's not something that happens a lot.

Ty was disturbed by this. He got involved, against the idea. He thought joining the group would be a terrible, awful, truly horrific idea.

"Oh don't do it," he pleaded. "Stay here. These guys have a real bad reputation when they go to bars. Real bad reputation... You should just stay here. They'll get you into trouble."

Ty seemed like a generally wise man, like he'd picked up a lot over the years, but he wasn't persuasive enough because a few minutes later, a group of us jumped in the back of Jason's pickup truck and rattled our way to The Irish Pub.

At the bar, as inhibitions became a little looser, reduced by whisky intake, I asked Jason what his dad had meant by 'bad reputation'.

He replied with a pause, a silence. A level of mystique and danger swept his voice. With intense eye contact, he looked at me.

"Well one time," he said, in a whisper, "we all went out to a pub just like this, and our friend Bill drank too much. He was caught by the cops urinating in some bushes."

8

Whisky and Being
Colin

IT TOOK 35 DAYS OF RIDING TO REACH THE FIRST CORNER OF
the route, which was the small city of St. Augustine in
Northern Florida. Everything had been going quite smoothly
overall. There had been just enough time to adapt to the unusual
way of life that comes with having everything strapped to two
wheels and some metal, and it was still early enough in the
journey to have a happy, gloss-coated mentality and outlook.

Almost all of the Civil War Reenactors had recommended
stopping in St. Augustine for the history. It was known as "the
nations oldest city" and had been founded in 1565 by a Spanish
explorer called Juan Ponce de León (also the guy who named
Florida). Legend has it that he stumbled upon Florida in his

search for The Fountain of Youth, which he had embarked upon because he was concerned about his aging. He died at 47 though so you could argue that he didn't succeed on his quest to live forever.

St Augustine was a beautiful city, but it was really more reminiscent of a small countryside market town in the UK, with old buildings separated by incredibly narrow cobbled streets. A local motel owner was really kind and offered to provide a room for a couple of nights for $30. This was especially rewarding as everything had become quite dirty whilst roughing it for the first month, and locking the bike and gear up in a safe place meant being able to walk around free and untethered.

It doesn't take long to grow used to looking after the bike like a small child, so when you don't have to monitor it constantly, it's incredibly liberating and often results in light-footed appreciative skipping down the city pavements.

As the night drew in, happy in the knowledge that the first section was complete, and after a long shower, I bounced to a pub. It's crazy how different your outlook is without the paranoia of feeling dirty and unclean.

The bar was dark, but not busy yet. It was awkward and took a little bit of plucking up courage to enter. Isn't it only weirdos who go to bars on their own? Probably.

I had rarely ever been to a bar at night on my own. It doesn't seem appealing at all. But America doesn't strike up the same 'solo intimidation' in my mind. Here, especially in places that aren't on the typical international tourist radar, you have the English accent to fall back on, which is often a conversation starter in itself, and can remove any lonesome awkwardness.

The bar began filling up. Hung on the walls were flashing Christmas strip lights that changed colour every few seconds. Christmas was coming up, just a week or so away.

Frank, a 70-something local, walked through the door with his entourage. He was rich. You could tell because he had a gold Rolex on. He was a whisky fan, in a generous mood.

I was sat at the bar and he came over with his wife and another elderly couple. When we got chatting, which was hard because of the blaring country music, he decided to purchase his gang and their newest member (me) some very pricey whisky. I don't know the brand, but a round for 5 of us came to $115. Crumbs.

It was impossible to pretend to be some kind of fine whisky connoisseur like the members of my new gang were, because whisky all tastes the same to me. I 'joked' about adding Coke to it, and they assumed it was a suggestion in jest.

We all drank a couple of drinks, chased with beer, and the conversation began flowing like the barrel taps just a foot away.

Conversation went quite well for a while. Frank had been a businessman, working in construction and based for years in Jacksonville, the city just to the North. He'd been living here since retiring nearly sixteen years ago.

However, it didn't take long for the pleasant atmosphere to change. Liquid generosity aside, Frank turned out to be a horrible man.

"They're taking over the USA too y'know?" Frank said, out of nowhere but passionately and with drunken rage.

"Who are?" I asked.

"The Muslims. Just like they are in UK," he went on. "I heard there's entire cities of Muslims and Arabs in London and they're forming a new government."

"Where did you hear that?"

"I have friends in London. They're looking to get outta' there. Their town has been taken over."

"Oh right."

"But I understand why they don't want to come here, y'know, because somehow America's ended up with a Muslim president from some place in Africa!" Frank shouted. "Kenya isn't it? How, I will never know. He's the anti-Christ! He's the devil! It's not how it used to be, even in the South. It's all changed in the last few years. There's going to be an uprising, I swear. They're gonna come after our guns and we won't stand for it. That'll be the start of it. More and more of us are getting sick of them. I'm stockpiling."

"Stockpiling?"

"Ammunition and Arms. I have a basement full. Gotta get supplies before Obama and his Muslim friends take 'em away."

"Wasn't Obama was born in Hawaii?"

"Yeah maybe, but who knows the truth anymore? There's a whole lotta' furore over his birth certificate. And either way, he's still a Muslim."

"Is he?"

"Yeah he is. Now what's with all the questions? I just bought you two whisky's."

"Oh right. It's just that I'm pretty sure Obama is a Christian, and there can't be entire cities of Arabs and Muslims in London, because London is a city."

"You know what?" Frank spat. "We just came in and thought as a Brit you'd understand. How dare you! We're American and this is our country. You want to see the real country? This is it."

He was fuming like a bull seeing red. This was the first time that I'd ever felt tension between an elderly man and myself. It wouldn't have been surprising if he'd taken a swing and that would've been unpleasant because you've gotta just suck it up and let a 70+ year old dude hit you in the face.

There was no swing, and Frank and his friends left.

In hindsight I regret being short with Frank and wish we'd spoken more, but with the gang gone, the night became much less intense immediately.

Socialising. Maybe it's worth addressing an elephant in the room so that it doesn't remain throughout this book. A guy leaves his home country to ride a bike for a year. What about relationships? I get it.

There are stories of people cycling around the world and meeting someone who they end up getting married to there and then, often in Vegas and dressed in Elvis costumes. At the back of my mind, I was not closed to that. Apart from the Elvis costumes. But it wasn't a search, and whatever experiences happened, well, happened. Eventually it became quite clear that you can either travel, or settle and meet someone, but usually not both.

If you've ever watched the film 'Love Actually', you know who Colin Frissell is. "I am Colin. God of Sex. I'm just on the wrong continent, that's all." He is the guy who doesn't have much luck with the ladies in the UK, so flies to Wisconsin, walks into a bar, and is immediately surrounded by three very attractive

Americans who proceed to be charmed with his accent every time he says a word like 'straw' and 'bottle', and then invite him back to stay at their house with a convenient caveat that they can't afford pyjamas so must sleep naked. And they can only afford one bed so they must all share.

This kind of scene might sound exclusive to Movieland, but I can assure you that in some parts of the US, the accent thing is truth. It happens. It is awesome.

So whilst I wasn't on an active search like Colin, I'd learnt about the benefits of being an Englishman in America from previous trips to the country, so perhaps when making the decision of where to go, as well as the mutual language benefit, that played it's part subliminally.

A big group walked into the bar, and took over the room with raucous, booming laughter which changed the mood entirely and was infectious. It was Christy's birthday party, her 24th, but it was her mum and dad that got things started. They came to sit at the bar whilst "the littleuns got rowdy."

Christy's mum, a glamorous blonde woman in her mid-fifties, could've been mistaken for a bit of a cougar. As the sparkles from her top glistened under the Christmas lights, she told me about how she went to the UK once and loved it. She'd worked in the US embassy on a transfer for 6 months in the eighties.

She shouted across the room and Christy came over.

"This is Dave," she introduced. "He's from England. Listen to him talk."

What did she want me to talk about? I was confused.

"England?" Christy asked, "no way! Where's a bar stool?"

It was an introductory scene that Colin Frissell would've been proud of, something straight out of Wisconsin. We ordered a few rounds of birthday shots. She had a nose piercing and a colourful tattoo on her forearm. I love tattoos. We were pretty much the same age. Maybe this was fate or something. Maybe Colin's theory about simply being in the wrong place was totally right. Maybe, I too was a God of Sex, now on the right continent. Right?

Christy really liked dancing, and she attempted to become a teacher of some basic Charleston steps. I drunkenly stumbled about, embarrassingly going through the actions for a bit, and hoping no-one was watching, before it being obvious to both of us that sitting down was probably a better plan. So, putting on our beer goggles, we went to a table and chatted about pretty much everything for a couple of hours, and then she leaned over, bit my earlobe and pulled it with her teeth. Raunchy. Maybe, she too could not afford pyjamas.

Early indications suggested that Christy wasn't the commitment, future-wife type, so we probably weren't going to organise an impromptu wedding, but possibly a memorable evening was being formed.

But, continuing the theme of being like a scene from a RomCom, just a moment later her boyfriend of 5 years walked in, with his motorcycle helmet.

Ecstatic to see him, she bounded across the room into his arms and kissed him in front of everyone for an awkwardly long time.

She could've mentioned her biker boyfriend of half-a-decade before the earlobe moment, couldn't she? I drank up and walked into the night, back to the motel.

9

Luke Warm
Christmas

FOR MANY PEOPLE, CHRISTMAS IS A TIME TO CELEBRATE
with family and friends. I didn't expect the festive period to
be as tough as it was.

For the first time, a rising sense of loneliness and isolation
began to overtake anything that was upbeat. People all around
were in their warm homes, enjoying themselves with their families, and I saw the glow of their living rooms from the distance
of the asphalt.

On the 23rd December I woke up early in the grounds of a
church in Blountstown, Florida. 7AM, and outside the unzipped
tent was the faint glow of a rising sun, still far from touching the
horizon to start the day.

The streets of the small town were lined with fairly lights, hung up between lamp posts. The notice board described events, special concerts, services. A big Christmas tree hung over the thin, dark river, with lights scattered amongst the thin branches.

On occasion, I would wake up early, motivated. On those days it was clear that the day ahead was going to be a big one. So far the maximum 'big day' had been a ride of 81 miles, back in New Jersey. Today, I knew that if nothing went wrong, this was going to be the first 'century day', a hundred miles or more. I was adamant that it be achieved before the start of the new year, and also wanted to do it purely to take my mind off it being a lonely Christmas.

Over time it became clear that simply making the decision to ride a triple figure day is the hardest part. It's very simple to do, you just have to endure the necessary time in the saddle. But I hadn't learnt that yet, and it felt like a faraway and oddly significant goal. Maybe doing a hundred miles would mean I would feel like a cyclist and not a fraud anymore?

The motivation for big days didn't come around that much because to cover that distance, unless most of the ride is downhill, you are really signing up to feel totally done in the next day, in pain, and sore. But it was nearly the 25th, and I planned on eating lots of incredible food, taking two full days off, and calling home.

Fort Walton Beach was up ahead, just over a hundred miles away.

Long, straight, flat roads through trees. They were beautiful at first but had become tiresome and monotonous quickly, because every day in this corner of the country involved the same thing.

That's where audio came in. It had quickly become a vital travel companion. Music for when you want to get fired up, podcasts for when you want to listen to stories or learn things or just hear other voices talking about normal stuff. Without audio, it is easy to fall into the 'loopy traveller who's gone turned into a nutcase' category.

It's peculiar how music, an album or even just a single song, can take you back to a specific moment. Meat Loaf conjures up images of that day in Florida.

"The sirens are screaming and the fires are howling,
way down in the valley tonight.
There's a man in the shadows with a gun in his eye,
and a blade shining oh so bright."

That's how I coped with the Floridian long, straight, flat roads through trees. Put the Bat Out Of Hell album on, and if there was no-one around, shout the entire album into the atmosphere as loudly as possible. If anyone had witnessed it, it would have surely been a strange sight, although little would they know it was actually playing a part in keeping me (relatively, maybe) sane.

"I can see myself tearing up the road,
Faster than any other boy has ever gone.
And my skin is raw but my soul is ripe.
No-one's gonna stop me now,
I gotta make my escape.
But I can't stop thinking of you,
and I never see the sudden curve until it's way too late.
I never see the sudden curve 'till it's way too late."

WAAAAAY TOOOO LAAAATTTTTEEE!
During the journey from East to West, there was regularly around half an hour when music wasn't necessary. At the end of the day, the sun would set directly ahead. Night after night, this moment of cycling towards the sun whilst it was sat at the end of the road provided tranquility. This golden moment was an escape from the newly developing dark trains of thought.

It was night, and that moment had long since gone when the trees opened to show the Gulf of Mexico. I was pedalling on a thin strip of land surrounded by water, exposed and being blasted by strong, salty winds. The lights of the city weren't far off, temptingly pulsing ahead.

At exactly 11.00PM, the GPS flicked from 99 to 100 miles. The day had seemed to take an infinitely longer amount of time than every other one, but the small accomplishment of ticking three figures seemed like a milestone.

What do you do when Christmas is coming, you've finished a hundred mile day, and it's nearly midnight? You go to a 24 hour waffle house and have a midnight dinner. Food had never tasted so good. Christmas was beginning to look up. Maybe that would be all it took.

A few hours later, on Christmas Eve morning, I woke up and glanced outside the tent into the grounds of another church. The rain was pouring, the ground was wet, my thigh muscles had seized up in the night and were excruciating. I stayed there for hours until the rain died off.

But the negatives were irrelevant because, soon, there'd be no need to move from a double bed and a long-desired turkey sandwich.

I arrived at a motel, bike in tow and bags under my eyes. No matter the length of sleep, a night in a tent isn't as refreshing as a night in a bed, and it's sometimes obvious. The few staff who remained, understandably wanted to be at home for Christmas. They were offering free cookies on the reception desk. Chocolate chip or raisin. The receptionist put 3 of each in a bag and handed it over, as though it was a secret.

I crammed the bike into the elevator, threw it into the clean room, took a shower, and then took a nap. This was home for a couple of days. There was no schedule.

Later, awake, all that was on my mind was Christmas dinner. That was important. Crucial in order to remain upbeat without company.

I bounded down the street, armed and ready to take an enormous turkey-based meal or four back to the room for the next day.

Around and around I walked.

There weren't many shops in this part of town. There was an open 'Whataburger' though.

The girl at the reception was wearing some Christmas accessories to spruce up her uniform. Her name badge said Rose.

"Hi, um, can I have the number 3, please?" I asked.

The number 3 was a 'Triple Meat Whataburger.'

"The number 3! Are you sure?!" Rose replied in shock.

"Yes please," I laughed, "why is that so shocking?"

"Well it's pretty big. There's three layers and a whole lot of fries... Most people go for a 1, or a 2... OK, I have an idea. Because it's Christmas, let's do a bet. If you can eat the whole meal, I will personally buy you a second one."

Big mistake, Rose. Big, big mistake. That is a flawed bet. If I had to describe, specifically, a demographic who could eat any size burger you throw at them, it would be those people who'd pedalled a long way the previous day.

The burger and trimmings were put on a tray. The challenge, on.

It took eight minutes to eat. I haven't really ever won much, so in my mind were flashing images of a caveman who had just discovered fire. Winner.

"I can't believe it!" Rose declared. "Here you go then. You want it to go, right?" Paper bag in hand, I left.

The supermarkets had closed. Surely there must have been something open, but I never found it, so gloomily walked back to the motel. Whilst it wasn't a turkey dinner, the mix of cookies and heated up burger would provide a unique festive meal.

Christmas day was deflating and depressing. It was really rubbish. I called home which was a highlight, and then lay around feeling sorry for myself. The microwaved burger was disgusting and soggy, and the cookies stale. There was a vending machine that did Snickers bars. Even that joy didn't last long.

100 miles to the West of Fort Walton Beach was Mobile, Alabama.

On Boxing Day, pretty excited that Christmas was over for one year, I loaded up the bike and took the elevator to the ground floor.

In the reception was a TV screen. The local news channel was on, showing the images of 'The Christmas Day tornado' that had happened late the previous day in Mobile. It was a wedge tornado, and had ruined a hundred buildings.

A receptionist looked down from the TV, to the bike, slowly putting two and two together.

"Which way are you going?" she asked, anxiously.

I glanced at the TV and said, also nervously, "To Mobile."

"You shouldn't go West. No way. You should go East."

If You Go Down
To The Woods

I T WAS A REGULAR ROAD.

Up ahead was a big truck. Behind it was another big truck.

They were on their side, I was on mine.

The second truck, at the rear, pulled out in an attempt to overtake the truck in front.

It was on my side of the road now, blasting at full-steam ahead. The driver high up in their seat, concentrating only on the overtake, not looking out for anything that wasn't as obvious as an oncoming car.

I kept pedalling, in the moment it seemed like the only option, although my nerves rose as we got closer to one another. There wasn't a good place to stop, no hard shoulder. The truck kept raging forwards, but they'd surely stop and get back in their lane.

Nope. As the driver ploughed forwards, he didn't see me so I steered sharply to the right, moving at a fair pace, hitting gravel, then grass, then a big mound of dirt, before eventually skidding to a stop, shakier than a few seconds ago.

The hurricane had fizzed out into nothing, causing no issues. It was the 28th December, and the city of Daphne in Alabama was approaching, just a few miles away.

Other than a single snapped chain and a few punctures, there had been no serious mechanical trouble for the entire month-and-a-half since setting off. Everything seemed reliable. The only variable to that reliability had been my fluctuating motivations. But when it came to the bike, so far it was keeping it's side of the bargain.

There is some simple stuff - stuff that doesn't seem like it would be a big deal to leave behind - that you end up really longing for. Before setting off, films were a staple part of my life. I severely craved locking up the bike and going to watch a movie with a sugary drink and a popcorn - which was weird because I wasn't pregnant.

'This Is 40' had just been released. It was a comedy. The GPS had the ability to search for any "POI" or Point Of Interest, all you had to do was type it in. I typed in 'movie theatre', set it to 'bike mode' and 'avoid freeways', and it came up with a route. It showed that the theatre was only a mile away. I'd probably be able to catch the next showing.

Trust the science. The GPS knows best. Those are two statements that you might think make sense.

It said to turn left off the main road, which led to some small, lit up Alabama streets.

"This is an odd way to go," a sensible person would think.

After a while, the streets ended and the alcoves began. Then a dead-end. Up ahead was a brown wooden fence with a gap in it that lead into some woods. Really thick woods. I rode through the gap, and started on a dark dirt trail. It was 6PM and was now completely dark.

The distance on the computer read only 0.7 miles away now, so even though it was a quirky route, it seemed to be working.

The trail was full of tree roots, rocks, steep downhill sections, dirt berms. It was everything a mountain biking trail should be. I turned the bike light to full beam mode. It lit up the trees like the Christmas branches of Florida.

In hindsight, the only problem with this situation was the bike. If it had been something built for the job, like a full suspension downhill bike, all would've been good. But it was a fully loaded, fully rigid touring bike, built for flat, regular roads.

The issue was: do you have a ton of fun and embrace the adrenaline, which is hard to come by when you ride slowly on flat roads, or are you sensible?

Of course the answer seemed obvious.

Everything rattled. I hit the dirt trail as fast as possible, speeding round the corners and trying to remember how to ride a mountain bike. The blood was pumping as I sat back over the seat to descend a loose rocky section. One shoe popped out of it's pedal as the bike leaned over to one side to go around a tree. The tyres became more and more clogged with thick, clay-like dirt, as the smile on my face got bigger and bigger.

Throughout all of this, I couldn't help but think it was an odd way of getting to the cinema...

But what a rush. I thanked the GPS for providing a thrill.

Towards the end of the woody descent grew the familiar tungsten tone at the end of a thin wooded tunnel section of track. And moments later, rolling out of the trees and onto the road, I didn't regret taking the trail for a second.

There was a street sign. Hold on... The road was the exact same one that I'd turned off. There had been no need to go through the woods. "Of course there hadn't," that same sensible person would think.

The strip mall lights were obvious from a way off, and the cinema was tucked away at the back. Sometimes there's an obvious sketchy vibe, but that wasn't the case here so I pedalled to the side of the cinema, found a subtle looking spot, locked the bike to some metal stairs, and went inside.

Relief. Laughter. Relaxation. The movie was a good idea.

A couple of hours later, I returned to the bike, happy, and began to unlock it. The rear tyre was flat, which, although annoying, was nothing unusual. It could wait. I pushed everything over to a patch of grass next to the road.

I woke in the tent the next day, to the sound of passing cars. It always seemed quite surprising how, even in the most obvious camp spots, more often than not nobody cared, and so it was possible to often literally just stop and put up the tent, without worrying about being hidden by trees or bushes or being out of sight.

That morning, whilst beginning to fix the bike, it was the first time I really noticed that gear was starting to take a beating. The tyres were bald, gears clunky, brakes squeaky. Luckily there was a bike shop was just around the corner. Time to replace the rubber.

"What width tyre do you want?" the mechanic asked.

"Erm. The same as what's on there now?" Yep, definitely still winging it despite triple figures.

The mechanic nodded and began to inspect the wheel. His eyes and hands followed the shape of the wheel, and then transitioned from 'totally normal' to 'there's a problem here'.

"Dude, the tyre is the least of your worries." He called across the workshop. "This rim is cracked in like 5 places. It's totally destroyed. I'm really surprised that you've got this far and it didn't collapse under you. Could've been super dangerous."

He pointed to the multiple spots on the rim where it was falling apart. You could pick at the cracks in the rim, and remove entire sections like a jigsaw puzzle. The spokes were tearing out of the wheel. It was destroyed. In fact it was so badly destroyed that it couldn't have possibly gone unnoticed for long, so clearly it was caused by bouncing between rocks and down a dirt trail through the woods. Whoops.

When it comes to loaded-down, long-distance biking, there are only a few things you should look for in a wheel. The obvious 'must' is getting one with a lot of spokes. 42 or 48. These are strong. The shop could've ordered one like this - a specialist wheel built for the job, like the Salsa wheel that had been working without issue until yesterday - but it would involve waiting for a week or more. So I bought the only suitable size wheel they had, a cheap 32 spoke one, aware that it would just be an in-between measure.

There wasn't much daylight left, so I got going with gusto in an attempt to get out of the city. The innocent white sky turned dark and intense. The clouds opened, like a scene from a cartoon, and it poured down.

11

From Short To Long

IS A TRIP LIKE THIS ACTUALLY REALLY SELFISH? IS DOING anything alone for a long period of time a form of selfishness? Those questions were stuck in my mind, encouraged by the passing of time.

There's a difference between short term and long term solo travel. Short term is mostly fun and games, a positive ball of joy, a vacation. Long term is none of those things. It has fun moments, but is also wrought with insecurity and doubt.

Why is this a good idea?

Is this in any way worthwhile?

Is it escapism because I'm too weak to handle 'the real world'?

It was in Louisiana when the first significant dose of inner darkness hit.

There was a storm that lasted for nearly an entire week, and when riding in the open, it could only be classed as 'scary as fuck'. Minute-by-minute, lightning surges lit up the sky like the Blitzkrieg. Bolts of hyper-electricity that instantaneously jumped from the dark and looming clouds to somewhere faraway, were blocked from view by the treetops either side of the road.

I should've been glad for the tall trees, knowing that in theory they were a lot more likely to receive any lightning than a person at road level, but in the moment it's impossible to think that way. All I saw was the rain pelting down like daggers which had now converted the surface below my tyres into a centimeter deep temporary lake. All I heard was the cracks of thunder that sounded just inches away. Touched by lightning, the entire road would become one big electric river.

I had to escape, so found a place to hastily unravel the tent in the grounds of a closed railway museum, in the rural town of Kinder, South West Louisiana.

Whilst the rain battered down onto the canvas, producing an erratic drumbeat of heavy droplets, I lay flat in my regular confines, as the self-doubt uncomfortably clogged my mind like tar. It hadn't done so before, not in a way that couldn't be quickly shaken off at least.

I had no answers to those questions. Not honest ones anyway. I didn't know why the hell I was here, or what on earth the point was, or whether it was just a different way of running away from the real world.

There was a mental juxtaposition regularly at play, of being "on a trip that people would give their right arm for." Several people had said that, which made the contrast an ever-present battle - a feeling in the dark moments of being depressed, yet knowing that, surely, it was wrong to feel anything other than joy.

I wondered how many people would be loving it if they were living it. Surely not many. When it all goes wrong, when the storms batter down, when you haven't spoken to anyone for days, when the dirt builds up, when things break, these are the things that add up to turn the short term into long term, the light into dark. These are the things which create misery.

Mike, a friend from back in the UK, had sent a message via my blog which I spent days in the tent thinking about.

"I have been wondering if you have seen any places where you have thought about holing up?" he wrote. "I guess one of the lifestyle choices that we all make is whether we are going to stay out on the road or if/when/how we decide to stick around in a place and make some relationships and put down what are usually called roots (I have never known what that has meant!). Asking people what they mean by 'home', or where is 'home' is an interesting question – is your home your bike at the moment, or is it the virtual world that you inhabit through your blog, or is it the place that you happen to be?"

In retrospect, I can better attempt to answer that question. It's a bit irritating to say that, for a long time, I felt a strong sense of validity in the 'trip' nature of the journey. The constant movement and momentum is something which in my eyes made it more real, the experience more authentic and respectable. Because of that, for the first couple of months I probably travelled right past a lot of valuable experiences, but at the time I was blind to another approach.

The answer to 'where's home?' was, in that tent in Louisiana, I didn't feel like I had one. The blog definitely played a big part in providing an outlet for creative expression and documentation, but it wasn't warm and it didn't have a kitchen. I had no home - it wasn't the bike, or the blog, and it wasn't the place I was, because that place had been new almost all of the time. Because of that, as the rain poured, I did feel like a hobo who'd drifted away from real life. Rootless.

The always-on-the-move approach was all ego. I now think a big part was immaturity too. I wanted people to know that I was hardcore, and could cope, and that the mental struggle had nothing on me. I wanted to prove that to anyone who doubted me, and surely this approach would garner more respect than a casual jaunt for pleasure. In my mind, the trip needed to be fucking hard work and a real slog on all counts - creatively, mentally, physically - and anything less was pointless. It needed to be an achievement.

I didn't tell a soul but a big part of that thinking was because I still felt some sourness about the split from the company I'd left prior to the journey. We'd built something together and now I needed to build something bigger on my own. I wanted to prove my worth, to onlookers and to myself. That was hardly a healthy recipe.

The doubts became annoying. Annoying like the documentaries where "professional adventurers" go on holiday and then cry all the time about it being too hot in the desert. Babies. Of course the desert is hot. I didn't want to be like that but being in that tent seemed like a fast-track to having a similar break-down. I don't like it when emotions take over, and have a few go-to-techniques to control them. Like in a sad movie that creates a lump in your throat - picturing the sound guy hovering a boom mic just out of shot with low jeans and arse crack exposed makes the movie seem less sad. Try it. Another technique is to stop wallowing and do something to take my mind elsewhere.

Originally the plan was just to pick up some supplies, but then I got chatting to someone outside a supermarket, and they said that just a few miles away was a huge casino. Casino? Casino + storm? Hmm...

Stumbling into the casino a couple of hours later, I was absolutely soaking. I unzipped my rain gear and handed them to a cloakroom clerk. He looked surprised. Apparently most people drive and don't arrive wet. But it was okay because they do really like to please you when you're at a casino.

I walked between the slot machines amongst the regulars, the people who do this all day, every day, and are addicted. The zombies. I had $20 but it's okay because I'd seen that film '21' with Kevin Spacey so was pretty sure I would make thousands in a few hours, and that would be a good investment for the journey funds.

"Would you like a drink, sir? On the house!" The waiter walked the floors taking orders, keeping the gamblers happy with a tray, finely balanced in his hand. I can't be sure, but if the casino management can make you a little tipsy, they probably benefit from peoples resulting liquid logic and willingness to have 'just one more go'.

Sitting at a slot machine, I chose one that takes quarters as a warm up. This would offer a few runs to get in the swing of things without burning through the $20 too fast.

Losing, losing, losing. The sound of nearby winners and coins being withdrawn was infuriating because the machines kept taking my money but not giving anything back. I had $9.75 now. Still time. $7.25.

What would Spacey do?

I spoke to the woman next to me, who was in her 70's. Her husband had died five years ago and ever since, she had "either been in front of a slot machine or asleep." She had pure white shoulder-length hair and wrist beads that rattled every time she moved to pull the lever. She seemed kind, like a trapped happy soul within the body of a ghost, now just focused on the lights and flashes of fruit machines, and only really communicating through the side of her mouth in between staring ahead. She said, through a whisper, that she didn't have any other family and this was home.

All the coins were gone. No more quarters and I'd not even had a chance to move on to the $1 slots. Screw you Kevin Spacey, look what you've done.

I sat down at the bar and watched Ultimate Fighting Championship (UFC). There was a final on. Knees, elbows, uppercuts, blood. There was a young couple at the otherwise empty bar too, called Tara and Jamie, and they were huge UFC fans. They explained that it's not actually as brutal as it looks, and no-one has died doing it, so after a while we were all simultaneously shouting at the screen. "Go on! Hit him! Kick him! Kill him!"

There was a band performing in a big room set off to the side of the casino so we wondered over. Laughter and awful singing. It was a blast and a stress-reliever, providing solace from the the transition from short to long term travel. The waiter from hours earlier was still walking around with his tray.

Two men came over. I'd not seen them before. They were dressed in black suits and were casino security. Serious people without much joy inside them, at least whilst at work.

"It's that time of night. You're not staying at the Casino hotel, and you haven't used the machines for hours, and you've just been drinking from the tray. Time to go."

The millions in winnings would have to wait. The tent would do instead.

The day after, back on the grounds of the train museum, I plunged into dark times again. Doubts. Made worse by a light hangover. And the fucking lightning still struck, and the rain continued to hammer down. Embarrassing self-pity and too much cursing. The realities of solo travel are not always jolly. It can seem a taboo to mention the dark times too much, but sometimes it can feel like a prison sentence. At times I imagined a judge with her hammer in the court room on sentencing day, looking down at me wearing an orange jumpsuit with both feet chained together.

"You are hereby imprisoned to twelve months of self-doubt, anxiety, and mental anguish," she'd say with a smirk, and then the prison guards would walk over and lead me away from the dock into the prison van as the chains rattled along the wooden floor. Then she'd say, "But remember, you wanted this." And she would be right. One reason why I chose this was because afterwards, it's always the tough bits that you look back on with the biggest smile. I'd learnt that from previous long-term rock climbing trips. But it was far, far harder to remember that whilst on a solo journey.

In the tent, though, interruptions from this dark train of thought were occasionally interrupted. The first time, on the first night, was the worst. But it didn't get much less shocking each time it happened. The end of the tent fabric lit up with a powerful light, getting bigger and bigger, brighter and brighter, and the sound of a horn got louder and louder, closer and closer.

Had I really been so stupid as to think the tracks here went unused? By the looks of the oncoming disaster just seconds away I wondered whether, in my haste to erect camp and escape the elements, this campsite was actually in the middle of the railway tracks? With enough sleep deprivation, your mind jumps to misguided conclusions. In just seconds, it seemed the train was about to plough straight through the tent destroying anything and anyone that got in it's way.

"Jesus Christ!" I roared to no-one, trying to slow my heart-beat, and catching a glimpse of the industrial train passing through rapidly on the tracks five metres away.

12

Prayers From The Fence

CAMPING OUTSIDE OF THE CHURCH SEEMED SENSIBLE until the Minister started screaming about guns from the depths of his office. It was relatively rare that I asked for permission to camp somewhere when it fell dark, but I saw a light on in the church office, so knocked to ask. It quickly became apparent that incognito may've been more suitable.

"Get away from the door! What do you want?!" the minister shouted from behind the door. That reaction is more under-standable if someone knocks on your door after midnight, but it was 7pm. "Do you have a gun on you?" he demanded to know.

"Um. No."

"I have a gun in here. On me right now. What is it? What do you want?"

"Erm. I just wondered if it would be possible to camp on the grass out here until the morning?"

After a minute or so of intense questioning, the Minister agreed, but throughout all this time, I didn't see his face, I only heard his muffled voice echo from behind the whitewashed door.

"And by the way," he said before finishing off what seemed like an unnecessarily intense conversation, "you really should carry a gun. Just a small one for self defense."

Texas is a unique place. Sometimes it seems trapped in the Wild Wild West, and other times it seems like a place on the cutting edge of innovation. There is a solidarity amongst native Texans too - a sense of a community united, of a state which could easily have been a country in it's own right. I got the impression that many Texans would probably quite like that.

It was January when I approached Navasota, in the East of the state. It's a small city of around 7,000 people, and is known for it's blues music, being named "The Blues Capital of Texas" in 2005. The cycle to this point, over the previous few days, had really offered the first taste of Texas. And important life lessons too, like never turning down a Texan barbecue. Oh crumbs, they are delicious.

Riding along, it was very easy to drift into a belief that you had gone back in time. A lot of people who ride a bicycle a long way talk about it providing the perfect speed, and it's really true. Put a motor in the equation, and you'll miss going through places like 'Cut And Shoot', a tiny town where all the buildings are in the style of saloons and you wouldn't glance twice at two cowboys walking out from the swing-doors, onto the dirt, and having a back to back shoot-out. Golden discoveries like these would be easily skipped at speed.

Navasota had the ingredients to be a standout experience. In the initial planning stages I had emailed a lot of city officials in places where I didn't know of any people to talk to, or where information wasn't easy to come by online. Emails were sent to mayors, telling them about the project, and cheekily asking "so who are some interesting folks in your town? Could you connect us?".

These requests were often greeted by a silence, but occasionally they would lead to some fun suggestions, and sometimes to a place even getting behind the journey. Navasota was one of those times, and up to now I'd been corresponding with Bert Miller, the mayor, who'd been helping with connections in the city.

Bert had got in touch with two people who he thought would be good characters to spend time with. On the first day in Navasota I was due to meet them. He'd lined up Misslette, a "professional singing cowgirl," and Stefan Smith, a "hog trapper."

Bert had also told a TV station about the journey and they wanted to do a story on it. This was the first dealing I had with press on the trip, and as someone who's only ever really been comfortable behind a camera, it was uncomfortable to be on the other side. However, part of this trip was about personal growth, and I wanted to use this as an opportunity to hopefully become a bit more confident.

On the first full day in the city, I rode down to meet Bert and put a face to the name. He was quieter and shyer than I imagined, which was a little different to the tone of the emails. He was friendly in a withdrawn way, but didn't have much time to chat, so had arranged for a city hall staff member to guide me to where he'd arranged for the introductions with Misslette and Stefan to take place.

We arrived, and Misslette the singing cowgirl was already there. She was dressed in full cowgirl attire. A hat, boots, you name it. I'd done a bit of research about her but hadn't come up with much, so went into the interview quite 'blind', which can work well sometimes and nosedive like a fiery 747 at other times. In the blind moments, I generally had some simple go-to themes and encouraged whoever was doing the talking to just riff on life. Such a vague approach can lead to a rare and un-rehearsed honesty, and it can feel like an oddly special bond is formed when people open up in this way.

"I love singing," said Misslette proudly. "See, when God gives people gifts... he gives us a talent, a gift, things that we're really good at, and we're to use those for His glory and to bless people. And He just so happened to give me the gift of music, and I'm very content. I love to sing. It actually feels good. It feels good physically, emotionally. When I'm through singing, I'm just so relaxed."

Misslette was a professional musician who specialised in Country and Western music. She'd been doing it for 44 years and a lot of her songs focused on horses, ranch life, and glory to God. On top of the music, she runs a ranch and is a dedicated Christian, so the themes she sings and yodels about come from experience and are clearly close to her heart. The conversation we had was one of openness and vulnerability. Misslette had gone through her fair share of challenges and I was struck by the specific moment that she looks back on as her moment of change, her darkest time.

"I could've taught Heathen 101," she said. "I was a shining example of a Heathen. I was raised in Houston, Texas, and as a musician you're always in the bars, and people just assume 'I'll buy you a drink' as putting money in your tip jar. And I went on the wayward path. I smoked cigarettes. I did all sorts of things that I'm not proud of. But when I was serious, I cried out to God. And I said 'If you are really God, prove it to me'. I would go to church and go to an alter call, and then I'd come back home and do the same things that I used to do. I had a horrible drinking problem..."

"And anyway, on September 28th 1992, at 7.10 in the morning, I was staring at my ceiling, and just thinking 'my life is just out of control, I can't quit drinking'. My skin would burn, my nose would burn. I would have to wake up and put liquor in my coffee. And I had cried out to God and said 'I need help. If you're real, help me'. And that morning, I heard the audible voice of God. And people can think I'm crazy all they want, but 20 years later I still haven't had another drink. And you know what He said to me? 'DO NOT DRINK TODAY', that's all He said. And it scared me to death."

During the time spent talking with Misslette, a cameraman called Shane from the local TV station had quietly walked in to capture footage for a story to go out later that night. Misslette was in tears as she spoke about this moment, and the room fell silent.

When we wrapped up, it was quite a sombre few minutes after what had just been said. She had told a story that she doesn't tell much and is still quite raw. It felt like an honour to see behind the curtain, one which covered a painful path to where she was now.

To lighten the mood, there were a lot of jokes being thrown around. I laughed at Misslette's joke until quickly realising it wasn't a joke at all. "Y'know Dave, I want to pray for you on your trip. You don't mind do you?"

Whatever view you take on religion, I found out that day (and would continue to find out time-after-time over the next 9 months) that the effects of believing in a God or Gods provide a lot of good to a lot of people, many of whom are the loveliest folks you could ever wish to meet. This was new to me, a real applicable lesson in the value of diversity and not being ignorant by jumping to judgement. It's easy in an increasingly atheist and agnostic society to think of dedicated religious followers as being whacko nutjobs. I thought that, and I'm glad that the journey provided an opportunity to destroy the preconception.

"Here, give me your hands," Misslette asked. When she saw the confusion in my eyes, she giggled, "We're just going before the Father. He created you, it's okay!"

"What do I do? Do I do anything?"

"Are you a believer?"

"I'm still not sure."

"Riding the fence?"

"Yeah, exactly."

She asked me to close my eyes, and prayed for about a minute, asking God to provide safety throughout the following months.

"Father, we come to you in the precious name of Jesus, and we thank you so much that we have the ability to come to you, because of the blood that Jesus shed on Calvary for us, and that he made a way that we can communicate with you."

Part of me thought it was ridiculous and another part thought it was very kind, but I couldn't keep my eyes shut for very long because I was aware of Shane and his news gear. I was paranoid that he was laughing at us, so I looked towards him, only to find his eyes shut, pointing the camera in our general direction. That's dedication - usually a cameraman has to look at what he's doing. Shane was a religious chap too, becoming lost in Misslette's words to big G.

"I lift up Dave to you Father," she cried out. "I plead the blood of Jesus over him Father. I pray a hedge of protection around him. You know his heart, you know what he's doing. It can be pretty dangerous out there Lord, so I just ask that you command your Holy Angels to surround him for protection."

Being surrounded by Holy Angels seems like it'd be quite nice.

"Father, I ask that your favour would rest upon him. That everywhere he goes, that he is met joyfully. Because your word says that you supply all of our needs, and you made him. You created him. Father, I ask that you touch his heart and show him as he's riding his bike and sees all the beautiful sunsets and sunrises and everything that you have created, that you touch his heart and let him know that you are real, and that you love him and are there for him."

However unusual I found this, there was some comfort in it. I wasn't about to become Born Again any time soon, but it made me realise that "believing" is a small part of the religious puzzle. The benefits are more than that, they are a comfort in going through life confident you're being looked after. For some people, especially those who have been dealt a tough hand in life, that kind of belief can be what absolutely vital, and the thing which turns lives around.

Misslette wrapped up. Amen.

"See, that didn't hurt! You're not bleeding are ya!"

13

Trigger Happy

STEFAN SMITH WORE A RED BASEBALL HAT AND DARK, Maverick-from-Topgun style sunglasses. He had an unusually firm handshake. And it turned out he already knew Shane the cameraman because they'd worked on segments in the past.

Stefan was a hog trapper which basically means that he finds rogue pigs and gets rid of them. There's a troublesome number of wild hogs in Texas, and they cause a lot of property damage. When someone in East Texas has a problem with a hog, Stefan gets the call.

The plan was going to be to talk to Stefan in much the same way as Misslette. But looking out the window of the bland City Hall room, that seemed like a mistake. The skies were blue, but most importantly, this guy was a hog trapper, a badass.

He mentioned that as well as trapping hogs, he has a shooting range. He's able to kill two-hogs-with-one-stone, because his clients just want the problematic pigs removed from their land - they don't really care what happens after that. So Stefan is then able to take them back to his shooting range, where clients pay to shoot moving targets and then take the meat home to munch on.

"You have a shooting range?" I asked Stefan naively. "We don't really have guns in the UK. But it's pretty big in Texas?"

"What are we doing inside then?" Stefan said in shock. "Shane, you got room in your car? Let's go to the range and we'll have him fire some guns."

It was on.

We arrived at the shooting facility, and Stefan had an idea.

"I was thinking on the drive over here," he pronounced to Shane, "that we should have Dave kill a pig. What do you think? We can make it look like I kill it in the edit."

This was the first I'd heard of killing a pig. Unless you're Stefan, a regular day doesn't start out with the expectation that you'll be killing a pig.

My stomach grew light and queasy as I remembered watching Babe. "That'll do pig, that'll do."

I couldn't kill. Part of me wishes I was more willing to do things like this, for the story, y'know? But there was not a chance that I'd be able to go through with it, so I admitted to Stefan that targets would be the most I could shoot today. That was clearly hypocritical bullshit, mind. If we're happy to eat bacon, shouldn't we be happy to kill the animal? Of course we should.

Nothing was killed. Instead, we all climbed into a small wooden shack that overlooked a long stretch of grass. At the end of the range were small metal frames, each containing a target. I imagined terrorists plotting a strike.

In the shack, Stefan spent time unlocking high security cabinets and eventually pulled out the three guns that we'd be using - a Desert Eagle .44 Magnum, a Marlin 30-30 rifle, and an AR-15 semi-automatic.

"I enjoy this so much, and it becomes addictive," Stefan opened up. "I get to meet a lot of people - farmers and ranchers

- and it's the first job I've ever had where, when you get there, people are glad to see you."

We'd all bonded enough now to the point where everyone was comfortable, so all three of us spent an hour firing the multitude of firearms and attempting to hit the targets.

"You're a true killer at heart!" Stefan joked after I hit the target with some beginners luck. I loved it, and was well and truly trigger happy.

We used the AR-15 first. It's a scary gun, because it's so toy-like. "Any idiot can do it," a former border-patrol agent once told CNN. It's highly accurate, yet features plastic components, and is very light to the touch. When fired, it just makes a quiet 'pop' sound. Like a bigger version of something you'd find in a Happy Meal but somewhat more deadly.

The pistol had a kick that sends your hand high into the sky once fired, as though you're really aiming at hot air balloons. And the rifle has a loud pump-action mechanism which can't help but make you imagine yourself as Bruce Willis.

At the time it didn't seem unreasonable to ask if maybe later "we could try hitting the target by diving sideways across the room and firing it one handed in mid-air like in Die Hard?" It was a question met by silence initially.

Yippee ki-yay motherfucker.

They looked at each other, acknowledging that the Brit was clearly having a great time but didn't know what he was doing, and Stefan replied jokingly with, "And this is our problem. People trying to be gangster!"

Later, I asked Stefan about what he meant when he joked about there being a "problem." What was the deal with guns?

"My father was a big hunter and fisherman. We did it together all our lives, and those are memories that I'll carry the rest of my life - the hunting and fishing times I had with my father," he reminisced from behind the dark aviators. "So the idea is to pass this on to my children, along with giving other kids the opportunity to come out and hunt and be successful and target shoot. What you're experiencing, you didn't kill anything, you're just target shooting, and it's a lot of fun! Having guns and so on, it doesn't mean you have to always kill something to have fun."

The shooting was incredible, what a buzz. It's obvious there are many positives. It engages your mind. You need to be calm and focus to be accurate. It takes skill. It takes slowing down your heartbeat and remaining calm. Stefan was so helpful and encouraging, and he couldn't have been more gracious taking someone he'd just met under his wing for a day. I was inspired. Maybe after this was all said and done I could be a sniper or a hit man, or just start preparing for the apocalypse like Florida Frank.

But the negatives are clear too. And unfortunately, the whole trigger-pulling affair came at an incredibly sensitive time. Gun violence was being discussed in every part of the country, at every minute of the day. A month earlier, the Sandy Hook elementary school shooting happened, where 20 elementary school children and 6 teaching staff were shot dead. In July that same year, a guy dressed as The Joker entered a screening of The Dark Knight Rises in a theatre in Aurora, Colorado and killed 12 moviegoers with an AR-15 - the big toy gun that is not a toy at all.

"Everything that's happening at the moment, with the gun laws and stuff, what is going on?" I asked.

'Gun-culture' was a hot topic and just 24 hours earlier President Obama had, for the first time in history, issued 23 executive orders as an attempt to reduce nationwide gun violence. The whole 'firing guns' thing was awkwardly timely.

"Well mainly, our forefathers put together the Second Amendment so it allowed us to bear arms to protect ourselves, from a variety of things, whether or not we're hunting or harvesting food, or protecting our homes or children, or protecting others," Stefan spoke with a deep passion.

"That's what it was put together for. It was also designed to protect ourselves from our own government, if it came down to that point, if they got off on the wrong direction. Kinda like what they're doing now - getting off on the wrong direction. So I want to have that option, and everybody should have that option. We've seen in other countries that don't have this option - they have dictators. That's how they're ruled. Our forefathers tried to design the constitution so that we wouldn't have a dictator..."

"Our issue is," Stefan continued, "and what you experienced this morning, is that this country was raised on a Christian belief, and even though we've had so many different cultures coming in, immigrants and so on, being Muslim and Buddhist and whatever, we're still a Christian-based country. So we'd like to see our government acknowledge this is what that is."

"The executive orders that Obama applied - I agree with most of 'em. The background checks, especially with the mental people. More education. More security in the schools. I'm all about that," Stefan began pointing to the weapons to demonstrate, "but when it comes to telling me I can't have this gun, or this gun, and this magazine in it, nah! That's not part of it. And so, what my fear is, is if we allow 'em to reduce a gun, or magazine, it gives them the stepping stone to take this, and this, and define everything else."

There are two divided sides in the debate. Pro-gun and no-gun. The pro-gunners argue about the Constitution, and the Second Amendment, and the right to bear arms. Which are valid points, but ones that often seemed to be infused with paranoia.

I'd been preached to multiple times by people who said they'd stockpiled ammunition and weapons and food rations. Some people saw a civil war coming on the horizon. There was a fear, a genuine tension about the government stepping over the line. And this view didn't seem restricted to drunk Obama-hating meth-heads - switched on individuals were subscribed to it too.

That said, none of that was on my mind. No. As the triggers were being pulled, Shane filmed what appeared to be a raving mad British man firing an AR15 as used in many mass killings, whilst talking about how "awesome this is." Looking back, it's not a proud moment to be broadcast on the news.

Stefan put the guns away and we called it a day.

On the way back to Navasota, we popped in to a local barbecue joint for lunch with cameras off. The Navasota Special - pulled pork and basically every other kind of meat you can imagine. Remember, you never say no to a Texas barbecue.

However, I now looked at bacon in a new way. One where I felt like a hypocrite. It was tasty though.

14

HoYoung And
Movies

S AT ON THE FLOOR OUTSIDE A GAS STATION JUST OUTSIDE the city of Del Rio in Texas, drinking some iced tea, I took a sip and, in the heat of the desert, let out a satisfied 'aaaahh' as though a Dr Pepper commercial was being filmed.

At times, this part of the country felt like the windiest on earth. Until Texas, wind wasn't a big deal at all, despite being warned several times that cycling the Southern Tier from East to West was the wrong way to do it. There were emails suggesting to reverse the route because "the headwinds are going to kill you."

The landscape involved the sand of Mexico's Chihuahuan Desert on one side and the sandy planes of Texas on the other.

That's a lot of sand, and combined with strong winds makes for an interesting mix.

On the road was a cyclist loaded up with four yellow and white panniers, a makeshift sand balaclava, and sunglasses to stop the sand getting in his eyes. It was clear that whoever they were, they were going a long way.

We bumped into each other on a bridge an hour later. HoYoung was from South Korea, and had been on an exchange for almost a year in the US studying business. He was planning on riding to California, and if he had time and money left, he was hoping to go to Las Vegas gambling and then on a Grand Canyon bus tour. He was loving it.

Later he told me that in South Korea, this kind of adventurous trip or extended journey is very rare and can sometimes be looked down upon, as it doesn't fit into the norm of going to university, starting a career and then having a family. There's a very strong workaholic culture that's drilled in from a young age there, and combined with very little vacation time and an obligatory conscription to military service, he admitted that this would probably be the last chance he'd ever have to do something like this.

HoYoung hoped to finish the journey and take his bike back to South Korea to eventually pass on to his future children, with a message of support if they ever wanted to go and do something that wasn't seen as normal.

He was the first rider I'd met who was also travelling in the 'stupid direction', and was the first person I spent a long period of time with during the trip. Over the next six weeks, we would often travel together and get destroyed by Texas and Arizona headwinds. I'd rip into HoYoung's love of Kelly Clarkson music and Heinz mustard, and he would rip into the state of the Premier League and my concrete belief that one day Taylor Swift and I would marry.

A bond was formed over those unique (and sometimes bizarre) experiences which can only be found when your life is strapped to a bicycle. Negative thoughts of isolation vanished, and I realised that one big secret to happiness is simply shared experiences.

As we made our way from Comstock to Langtry in Texas, gravity stopped working. It's no surprise that after a long time spent riding uphill, it's exciting to see a huge downhill section of road. These are often the best parts of the day, a relief when you can sit back, relax, and freewheel. That excitement disappears when, as soon as you stop pedalling, the wind causes you to stop moving entirely, no matter the gradient.

It's hard not to become a bit numb to your surroundings when slowly travelling over a long period of time. But every so often the world goes snap and your jaw drops and nearly shatters all over the floor. We crossed the Pecos River bridge. The deep gorge of orange tufa-covered limestone hanging above the river, and the shimmering emerald green water below pushed away any numbness.

In a twist of fate, we were riding on a long, deserted and straight stretch of road. One of the ones that just goes on and on into the distance. HoYoung was 200 metres in front and we were both plugged into headphones with music on loud. I'm not sure what he was listening to but it was probably Kelly Clarkson. "She's motivational." Of course she is. A pickup truck came from the other direction and pulled up next to him.

Communication could be challenging for HoYoung. His English was good, but he still had trouble understanding conversations occasionally. That was made harder in this part of the country because a deep, rural Texan accent can be hard enough for a native English speaker to understand at the best of times.

The pickup driver was someone who had worked on a farm in the area, and he recommended that we stay there to escape the wind. He said that it was a popular place to stay for cyclists on The Southern Tier. It sounded like a good idea but when I reached HoYoung he laughed because he had absolutely no idea what directions the driver had said.

We were carrying cycling-specific maps from the Adventure Cycling Association. Each one lists accommodations in the area and provides the contact details to ring ahead. I nabbed HoYoung's phone and called the campsite listed on the map. Someone called Tom said they were open and they'd be expecting us in a few hours. It turned out to be the same farm that the pickup driver had advised.

When we met Tom, a grisly looking biker with a dark ponytail and a denim jacket covered in embroidered patches, the sun was dropping and there was probably around 45 minutes of light left that day. Without an introduction, and as though we'd known each other for years, he quickly said "Ah about time guys, let's grab a few cold ones. I wanna show you something."

We piled into a 4x4 and went off-roading. We were being thrown from side to side inside the vehicle when Tom told us what he was doing here. He was a recent retiree from Minnesota who had been stationed at the farm for the last month, fixing up windows, making shutters and generally helping out on the farm in return for free accommodation in a trailer. He was a cross-country motorcyclist, so understood what the appeal was of being on the road.

We drove to the edge of the canyon that overlooked the Rio Grande - the river which is the border between the United States and Mexico. Tom was eager to share the local knowledge that he'd picked up during his time on the farm and took us to a secret split in the canyon which you can throw a rock into and it will fall all the way to river level.

Each of us cracked open a beer and sat at the edge of the drop, occasionally throwing rocks into the abyss. We probably all hoped no-one was a psychopath with a penchant for pushing people off edges.

We spent half an hour listening to Tom's motorcycle tales and watching the sun drop below the horizon, and in a rare moment of stillness and no wind, the sky transitioned to a bright red glow in the sky over Mexico. It was the kind of moment that is hard to forget, and I wondered whether this would be something that HoYoung would tell his future kids about when he passed on his bicycle. It is certainly a scene I will be telling to Taylor and I's future children.

When we returned later that night to the main campsite, there was a tent on the grass outside Tom's trailer which hadn't been there a few hours ago. From inside, we heard loud snores. Other than HoYoung and I, there were no registered visitors staying on the farm, so Tom wanted more information on who it was. He shouted out in the direction of the snores.

"Excuse me. Hey. My name's Tom and I work here. Is there anything you need?"

"No, I'm OK, thanks," replied the tent in a worn and entirely irreverent voice.

"How long are you planning on staying?" asked Tom.

"Just tonight," the tent explained.

"No problem. We're probably going to make some dinner and watch a movie in the trailer if you want to join us?"

"No," the tent said, abruptly ending an already awkward conversation.

That was the last we heard from the mysterious voice in the tent. We found out the next day that he was a cross-country hitchhiker, and had been picked up and driven for a couple of miles by the same driver who'd stopped to talk to HoYoung. He apparently wasn't very friendly, kept himself-to-himself, had troubles on his mind, and "could've done with a shower." Couldn't we all?

I set up the tent, bundled everything inside and headed into the trailer for an impromptu night at the cinema. What movie do you think of when you imagine something a hardcore, leathered-up motorcyclist would want to watch? I thought it'd be something epic like Easy Rider. Or maybe something with gun battles, like Black Hawk Down. Maybe The Godfather.

So it was quite amusing when we decided on which movie to watch. And it was definitely the right choice because out of everything in the movie collection, this film was definitely the easiest to understand regardless of any language barriers the viewers may have.

For the next 90 minutes, us three rugged and manly cross-country bikers sat together in a cramped trailer with some pasta bake, giggling like children to Mr Bean The Movie.

15

A Cell And Juarez

I WAS SAT IN A CELL NEAR LAS CRUCES, NEW MEXICO, GOING out of my mind. There were bolts on the floor, a thick metal door and a bullet-proof window. It had been 99 days and now it looked like the journey was over. The US Government were talking about putting me on a plane and booting me out of the country.

How had it come to this?

The cell was usually a place for Mexican drug cartel members. They'd get detained here before being arrested or being kicked back into Mexico. Southern New Mexico sees so much drug-related activity because Juarez is just 50 miles away. It's a city which, due to cartel-related homicide, make it statistically "the most violent place on the planet that's not classified as a war-zone."

Being in this cell was not part of the plan.

A few hours earlier, things were different. Over a couple of light days in the saddle, I'd left Texas and entered New Mexico - The Land Of Enchantment. Life on the road felt great and it was a troublesome-free time. It would not be a stretch, in fact, to call it, um, enchanting.

Hatch is a small town in the South of the state, within 100 miles of the Mexican border. It was the final place I reached before being put in a cell built for drug dealers.

The area surrounding Hatch is known for it's infamous green chili farms. The roads were flat, long, straight and empty. It was quiet, and a perfect time to fall into a trance of movement. Things were good and had potential to get better, because everyone kept talking about the chili burgers in Hatch, and you know now that I am a burger fan, as long as they're not microwaved.

Because of the close distance to the Mexican border, there are occasionally US Border Patrol checkpoints. They are simple road blocks with an attached Portacabin office. Their purpose is to check that everyone on the roads in Southern New Mexico has all the official documentation and aren't illegal aliens or up to any Walter White and Jesse Pinkman funny business.

I cycled up to the checkpoint gates at around 11PM without thinking about it at all. A check of my passport would reveal nothing extraordinary, and other than a perhaps slightly dodgy looking beard, I didn't think I looked much like a Mexican drug dealer.

"Passport please," Maria, the US Border Patrol Officer, asked. She was tall, dressed in a green uniform with a clip on radio and a pistol, and seemed very standoffish.

"No problem, give me a second to dig it out."

It was late, and chilly, and understandable that Maria wanted to be inside the Portacabin rather than outside.

"Oh don't even worry about it," Maria responded with frustration, "go ahead."

"Oh here it is," my words came almost instantly after hers, "here you go."

Maria switched on her flashlight, pointed it to the photo page, looked up and then back at the photo, and handed the passport back with an unenthusiastic tone and a nod to continue.

"Could you tell me what date I need to be out of the US by?" I asked, in what is now an obvious moment of madness.

"Sure, let me run it through the computer," Maria replied, perking up at the thought of going inside.

I parked the bike outside the Portacabin and followed her in.

Behind two desks were Maria's colleagues. Ron, a stick thin man in his 50's, sporting a archetypal law-enforcement mustache exactly like Ron Swanson's, and Tom, a stocky guy in his late 20's who, unlike the others, seemed as though he hadn't become jaded by the job yet.

Maria went over to her computer with my passport. I sat down near to Ron and Tom. They were intrigued by the situation, because they didn't see many people pass through here that weren't sat inside a petrol-powered metal box of some sort.

We chatted for a few minutes and they asked a lot of questions - in a friendly way rather than a law-enforcement way. After asking them how many people they'd shot, to which the answer was, "depends if you count the stun gun," I ran them through the route, told them about what had happened so far and what the plan was going forward. They seemed into it. They obviously didn't get many cross-country cyclists, and were keen to know more. Tom went to my website and started looking through all the blog posts and watching the videos. Then a voice at the other end of the room interrupted all fun and games.

"You're 9 days overstayed," Maria said bluntly.

"What do you mean overstayed?" I replied, confused.

"It means what I just said. You've outstayed your visa. You're here on a 90 day tourist visa, and it's been 99 days."

"What about the B2 page in my passport?"

I'd messed up. When a foreign citizen flies into the US expecting to stay for more than 3 months, they need to explicitly state to the Customs Official that they're here for an extended period of time, they're not on the normal 90 day visa, and they need to ask them to stamp the B2 visa exclusively. I hadn't known about or done any of those things. On arrival I had just showed them the passport and walked through.

"So what does that mean?"

"We have to send you home. We'll put you in an immigration camp until the next available flight back to the UK." Maria cut to the chase. What a kick to the balls. It seemed like there were no options.

"A couple of minutes ago you were waving me through and telling me to get going? Can we not just go back to that moment and forget this ever happened?" I half-joked, the motive quite serious.

"No. We've seen you now, we've run you through the computer. Sorry, but we can't."

A few minutes went by with silence. The officers were tapping away at their computers, and I wasn't sure what was happening. They'd given me a microwaveable burrito and orange juice. I'd love to pretend that the situation meant I'd lost my appetite, but that's not true at all.

"Maria, can I have a word?" Tom walked over to the other side of the room, "Can't we call Joseph at HQ and see if we can figure something out? We were just on this guys website and it looks legitimate."

A few minutes later, Maria got off the phone with Joseph, her supervisor.

"Don't get your hopes up. But there might be something we can do. I want you to go outside and dismantle your bike so it fits in the back of the truck. I'm going to drive you to HQ in Las Cruces."

We were moving. Maria was blasting down the freeway and getting irritated that there was no music that she liked on the radio. She didn't say much, other than that. We arrived at the HQ in Las Cruces, and she ushered me into the cell whilst she talked to Joseph.

Minutes passed. Then an hour. Then two hours. I sat there, looking at the clock ticking away slowly. Life in prison must suck.

The door opened. Maria walked in.

"I've chatted to the boss," she said, "and we think there's something we can do. But it's not exactly official. We think we can re-issue you with another 3 month visa stamp if you go to Mexico and then walk back over the border back into the United States. I'll drive you to the El Paso side and you can walk over to Juarez."

Maybe things weren't that bleak. Although, you never know, because this was Juarez we were talking about. The most dangerous place on Earth for journalists. With drug gangs who love to murder in the most gruesome way possible, and they don't care who they kill - it could be other gangs, or witnesses, politicians, news teams, it really didn't make a difference. In fact, Mexican gang murders account for 10 times more deaths than that of American soldiers killed in the wars of Afghanistan and Iraq. So there was an undertone of worry thrown into the equation too. But mostly a renewed optimism.

We were on the move again, and I was becoming more and more familiar with the back of the truck. Maria remained irritated that the radio stations were "playing shit." It took about an hour to reach El Paso, back in Texas.

At about 3AM, we stumbled in to the building at the border. It's a memorable scene when you walk in - you follow a claustrophobic and thin wire-lined tunnel for 20 metres. Maria guided me down the tunnel and into the main building, and started chatting to the Customs Officers.

They're a different setup to the Checkpoint Officers, and the communication between the two groups had been non-existent up until this point.

For a moment it was tense again, and there was doubt whether this plan was going to work after all. It took several heated discussions for the Customs Officers to agree, and they weren't happy about it.

"Listen, I'm just doing what my boss says. It is what it is," Maria shouted to a Customs Officer. Clearly she was blunt to everyone which was nice to know.

"It is what it is? It's bullshit is what it is! He should be deported. Get him stamped then, but this isn't cool at all," the officer snarled viciously.

I was unsure of the ins and outs of what had just happened, but 10 minutes later, a very pissed off Customs Officer stamped the page of my passport from behind his glass box, and I was back in the USA, topped up with another 90 days of freedom.

We left, with success under our wings, and walked back out of the claustrophobic wire corridor.

Maria was leading the way, and at the other side of the tunnel, walking towards us, were 20 guys in orange jumpsuits and handcuffs. There was a single officer at the front and a single officer hanging back at the end. The group was getting kicked back into Mexico.

I noticed Maria tense up, which was contagious and worrying. She raised her head, hovered her hand over her Heckler & Koch pistol and walked fast, looking straight ahead.

Most people in a jumpsuit had their eyes on the floor, kept themselves to themselves, and looked depressed. But two of them didn't keep themselves to themselves. They fixed their gazes upon us as we passed, their heads tracking us, and suddenly jolted their faces towards ours to try and scare us. It worked, I was terrified. But little did they know, no-one can scare Maria.

We were back in the truck, driving back to the checkpoint. Maria once again complained about the local radio. I wondered why she didn't just bring her own CD's.

"Mind if I smoke?" she said.

'Really?' I thought. 'You've just saved my bacon, do whatever you want. Turn this truck into an industrial chimney if it makes you happy.'

Staying and carrying on was all thanks to Maria.

16

The Way Of The Apache

SOME NIGHTS ARE TERRIFYING. NOT FOR ANY REASON other than lame things like the wind and rustling noises, but they're scary nonetheless.

I woke up. It didn't seem like there'd been much sleep involved. I'd been on edge the whole night, to the point where I had a tent peg tucked into my sock, and a knife under my drybag-pillow.

Nothing happened, of course. There was no need to get all Keanu Reeves on anyone. So it's a bit of a pointless story really. I suppose if there's a point, it would be that sometimes nights camping in new places are scary, because you don't know what's there, but there's probably nothing to be scared of.

HoYoung and I had ridden on different routes a couple of days after the Mr Bean movie night, and we'd loosely arranged to meet again a week or so after. Turns out we didn't bump in to each other again for another three weeks, when we planned to team up and tackle Arizona.

It was the morning and I set off riding from Safford in The Apache State, Arizona. It's a state that's one of the most beautiful and underrated. Sparse, and with mountains that are sharp and looming.

The previous day had been a very physical one. There had been several intimidating climbs which passed through the Gila and Apache National Forests. One of those hills was a snake-like pass that carved up a huge Arizonan hill in the distance, and it was impossible to see where it ended. All there was to go on was the reputation of "the mountain" from locals.

Climbing those kind of hills is therapeutic in a way, because you don't know where the end is, so can't focus on finishing. You settle into a calm routine of ultra slow, granny-gear pedalling whilst tuning out the end. Before those type of hills began, I would always be hit with dread, but 5 minutes into them, the flow would start, like a deep meditation.

Sat on the horizon, on the road out of Safford, were some extremely dark storm clouds. Dark grey swirls seemed to grow in intensity every time my eyes drifted up from the concrete view just ahead of the front wheel.

It's not all bad. Weather changes, like the impending storm, can at times be hugely refreshing. They jolt you back into remembering that an experience should be varied and never too easy for too long.

A cyclist called Jeff was riding in the opposite direction, the 'sensible way'. There is always quite an amusing moment when you meet cyclists coming in the other direction. It's the 'secret handshake', when one of you crosses to the other side of the road and waits for the other to find out what they're up to.

Jeff was cycling from California to Florida, and was heading to meet his son in Texas. He'd been making fast progress and was just 8 days into his trip when we met. He beamed friendliness, and unlike a lot of the fast touring cyclists, he seemed to be loving it for what it was instead of how fast it was taking.

The reason he'd gone a long way was not that he was a fast mover, it was just that the guy had grit, enjoyed being out in nature, and could endure more saddle time than most.

"It's funny," he said, "you're one of only two bikers that I've met going East to West, and the other one was only about two hours ago!"

"Oh cool. Do you know the other persons name?" I asked.

"I don't remember. Hold on let me just check on my phone, I made a note. He was from South Korea and heading to California."

Jeff didn't need to dig through his notes, I was pretty certain who it was. So far, the road heading West hadn't been full of South Korean cyclists.

HoYoung had a consistent riding routine which involved setting off early and finishing early, so if he was two hours ahead we were likely to bump into each other today.

My routine was often a, um, "relaxed" one. It frequently involved a slow start to the day. I'm a zombie in the mornings, and am far more of a night owl, so I'd typically spend a couple of hours packing up, eating and drinking, and gradually pluck up the motivation to leave at midday, stopping a lot along the way, and riding by bike light into the night.

About 60 miles ahead was San Carlos, a small roadside town which is at the head of the nearby Indian Apache Reservation, which is the tenth largest Indian Reservation in the US, and home to 9,000 people, a casino, and wilderness areas.

Dark, ferocious clouds loomed on the horizon. Mile after mile, the cold chill came - you know, the one that comes right before a storm. I reached a Texaco garage, went inside for a muffin, and returned to see that the clouds had opened and it had started to rain. There was a bench outside the gas station, protected by a shelter, so I sat there for a while. A local called Douglas from the reservation came over and sat down. He had a long ponytail, wore a brown leather waistcoat, and had leather cowboy boots on.

He talked about life on the reservation, and about how, whilst it's apparently referred to as "Hell's Forty Acres" because of poor environmental and health conditions, the people are kind and there is a strong sense of community. He described how he was disappointed that local education doesn't focus on teaching the traditional Apache language to children anymore, and so a huge part of history and culture will become non-existent within a generation.

As we spoke, the rain intensified and changed to heavy snowfall. It was a stark contrast to what Arizona had been so far. Douglas witnessed the snow and turned towards me and, with a tone of surprise in his voice and a hint of liquor on his breath, he said, "they said it was going to snow. It's the first time it's happened here for 6 years."

A Texaco worker came out to the bench and told us that there had been some road closures up ahead, in a town called 'Top-of-the-world'. I put on waterproofs, gloves, overshoes, and wrapped the Brooks leather saddle with two bin bags.

Douglas and I shook hands to say bye. He gripped my glove tightly, whilst staring intensely into my eyes and then looking out into the now snowy night with a worn, rugged face that had clearly witnessed a lot.

"The only way you'll survive out there, man," he advised, "is to follow the way of the Apache's."

It was hard to know exactly what he meant, but following the way of the Apache's seemed a little dramatic.

The snow intensified as I climbed and rode into the storm. The winds picked up and a small blizzard engulfed anything on the road. I had to stop and fumble around to find a balaclava. The bike-light was set to the most powerful setting, but the falling snow caused a reflection, so visibility was no more than 10ft ahead. There were no cars on the road. It was desolate, and 'out there'. I couldn't reign in the huge grin that started to form on my face. It's all about perspective. This was what it was about.

At 11pm, I descended in to the small city of Globe, following the line of streetlights. And there it was again, like it regularly was. The big yellow M of McDonalds, a haven of connectivity,

warmth. A place to hijack wifi. A haven that the Apache's probably didn't have. And HoYoung had just left a message.

"Did you set up your tent?" he asked. "I'm in Globe. I'm in
motel again. Because of the bad weather."

"You're kidding. Snowy out there. Saw Jeff earlier and he
said he'd bumped into you."

"You can stay with me. Keep going down hill. Wait, I will
check the name of this motel... Motel name is Elray motel. It is
right side. It is room 6. See u soon. Just do not pass the front of
the office hehe."

Serendipity perhaps. When I got to the motel, HoYoung's
stove was on in the corner, heating up noodles. He was a
funny and warm-hearted guy, and rushed to the stove, picked
something up, and came back to the door as I balanced the bike
against the wall.

"Want these?" he beamed. "I got them free from Walmart,
but have many extra."

Then he handed over three mustard sachets.

We set off the next day with a concrete destination in mind.
A couple called Gerri and Bill, both keen cyclists, had emailed
offering us a place to stay at their retirement home at a trailer
park in Mesa, just outside Phoenix. It was 72 miles away, over
what looked like some very steep terrain, so it was shaping up
to be a long day.

As we pedalled seemingly up and up, Arizona became more
spectacular. 16 miles of non-stop climbing brought us to the
mother of all descents. If I had to choose a single moment over
the entire year and give it a 'best downhill' trophy it would be the
one in Arizona. The road carved through a bronze, steep-sided
sandstone canyon. Two natural walls either side. A beautifully,
violently steep road.

We set off from the top and after a few seconds were at
maximum speed. There's nothing to do at that point other than
let gravity do the work. We whizzed down, carving around
corner after immaculate corner, through tunnels and over
bridges that spanned the gorge below. WEEEEE. After 8 miles
it leveled out in a small town called Superior. A glance back

towards where we'd come meant tilting our necks upwards to try to pinpoint the beginning of the road in the distance.

There's no denying it, try as you might. The ultra-short hiss was very loud. The sound of a nail going through an inflated inner tube. Every time that happens, it's hard not to get angry because you know the next 20 minutes are going to be oily and frustrating. But the noise came from HoYoung's wheel. Sucker.

He'd already stopped and turned the bike upside down.

"You have tyre patches?" HoYoung asked.

Sometimes a month goes by with no mechanical issues. Other times you can't go an hour without something going wrong. It's very frustrating when that happens. A new crunch, a snap, a creak, a puncture, a crack, you name it and in those bad periods it becomes far too regular.

Thankfully, in mechanical terms, the last couple of weeks had been good, but because of that, both of us had become completely complacent. All thoughts of carrying spares had faded. Neither of us had a spare tube, and when HoYoung started to apply repair patches, it became obvious that there was a lot of holes in his tube. We found the sixth hole after applying all 5 spare patches we had between us.

None of the bodges worked. We tried duct tape. We tried putting a knot in the inner tube.

When we realised that it wasn't going to work, HoYoung put out his thumb, and ten minutes later he bundled the bike in the back of a white pick up truck and headed towards Gerri and Bill's place.

And he was never seen again.

Just kidding.

I arrived in Mesa at 8pm that night and rode into the trailer park. Bill came outside and was instantly jokey with a "what time do you call this?"

Gerri and Bill had both done a bunch of long-distance riding, so they understood that struggles and setbacks were commonplace. They'd helped HoYoung to fix his bike and gave him a spare tube, and his bike was now running slicker than ever because of their handiwork.

Retirement villages are strange places. Gerri and Bill gave us a guided tour of the grounds. It felt a bit like a theme park for the elderly.

My stomach was rumbling like crazy the whole time on that tour, but I wasn't too concerned because in our emails Bill had asked whether I was a vegetarian, so I just assumed that meant a meal might be part of the evening. This was often a great part of staying with a host, we'd share dinner and stories.

Maybe he couldn't hear the deep roars of my stomach, because a few minutes later Bill offered an almighty blow.

"Sorry Dave, we didn't know if you'd show up at all, so we ate dinner earlier."

You've gotta be genuinely appreciative when someone offers a warm floor to crash on. That generosity is a sign of kind-hearted people. But gee whizz, was I hungry. A long, drawn out, dramatic and echoey 'NOOOOOOO' rattled through my thoughts.

Gerri, Bill, HoYoung and I spent the next hour jumping between the swimming pool and jacuzzi. It was a memorable setting. In the jacuzzi was 6 other people who lived here too. HoYoung and I seemed to be the only people under 60 years old, so we definitely stuck out, but everyone seemed welcoming and happy to see some younger faces. Especially one of the older women, Barbara, who would sometimes wink across the bubbly water at the two of us. Cheeky minx.

Everyone in the jacuzzi told stories. Gerri and Bill were planning to ride from Seattle to the East Coast that summer. Try as I may, as people told these tales and their plans and dreams, my mind would often drift to food. And the damn on-site shop was closed.

Was it just a mirage? I got out of the jacuzzi and walked over to find out.

No, maybe it was real. It was! It was real!

Slotting a dollar coin into the machine, I heard it fall. And then I put my hand into the hole, and felt it. The Snickers bar at the foot of the resort vending machine.

Suddenly I could think again, so stumbled back to the jacuzzi, content and with chocolate crumbs around my mouth, to get winked at by Barbara a little more.

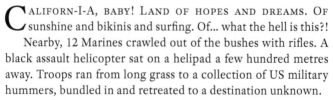

Cherish It

CALIFORN-I-A, BABY! LAND OF HOPES AND DREAMS. OF sunshine and bikinis and surfing. Of... what the hell is this?!

Nearby, 12 Marines crawled out of the bushes with rifles. A black assault helicopter sat on a helipad a few hundred metres away. Troops ran from long grass to a collection of US military hummers, bundled in and retreated to a destination unknown.

Somehow I was passing through what seemed to be a scene from the movie The Expendables. Rockets going off and bazookas being fired and huge explosions wouldn't have been out of place.

This was Camp Pendleton Marine Corps Base and it was massive and filled with obstacle courses, wire fences, tanks. Public roads go right through it, and take you away from the busy highway into the countryside, and with the right timing, you can find yourself surrounded by military training exercises that make you wonder if a war has begun and you've not been paying close enough attention.

Leaving the perimeter of the base on the new mission of heading North, I pedalled along the coast to the suburbs of the obviously affluent Orange County. Two frat boy bros stopped their black Range Rover, and the darkened windows descended to reveal their faces hidden by dark sunglasses.

"Hey dude?" the guy called across the empty road. I stopped riding, unclipped and figured he'd ask for directions or something.

"Nice pants, retard!" he shouted, followed by "Fuck off with your bike!" Then he quickly rolled up the window, in hysterics, and sped off. Dick.

So it wasn't the smoothest of starts up the new coast, and it might sound weird but small moments like that had the power to knock my confidence for a while. It's easy to let insecurity in when you're on your own and almost always tired.

Crikey though, what a relief it was to be next to the coast again. The ocean has a way of providing calm. Maybe it's the sounds, or the rhythm, or the vastness. It's all starting to sound a bit airy fairy now, so let's just say that being near the ocean was uplifting as it always is, and I spent a lot of time in the water, not riding anywhere.

For a few days I'd been emailing back and forth with Samira Mostofi, a film and TV assistant at Twentieth Century Fox, lining up an interview which I'd been looking forward to for, um, 6 years, kind of.

Riding through the heavy-traffic from the coast at Long Beach, passing busy neighborhoods that followed the LA River, and darting from road to sidewalk intermittently depending on the regularly stopping buses, I made it to Pasadena with plenty of time to spare.

There was an excitement in the air. As I walked onto the set at City Hall, trucks, cranes, balloon lights, and a hundred or more crew members were scattered around. This was where a new TV pilot was being filmed, and kicking around somewhere was Ruben Fleischer, the director of the episode and the guy who I was due to meet.

To explain a bit of the backstory, one of the reasons for being in Pasadena actually went way back. 6 years before this, I'd finished school and was deciding what to do. At that time there was basically two options that sounded exciting, and both of them revolved around film. One was to enroll on a film course, and the other was to try to get an apprenticeship with a filmmaker and learn the practical ropes from them. Nothing else seemed appealing at all.

At that time, there was a director who had a blog at ruben. fm. He'd made a bunch of comedy videos, music videos and commercials and I followed the updates on the site. It was kind of crazy to witness the transition that followed through updates on an unassuming blog.

One casual update, after the writers strike in 2008, read: "Luckily I have a lot of great projects brewing, and we can now really bare down and get to work. This year has the potential to be a big one, if these things come together. I couldn't be more excited. Onwards and upwards, it all starts now!"

Later, hints about starting to work on a new feature film called Zombieland appeared. And it gradually went from low-key updates about location scouting, to there being photos of a hundred zombie extras. When the filming wrapped, and the movie was released 8 months later, it exploded. Ruben had just directed his first national #1 box office hit, and he was right to think that year was going to be a big one. Since then he's directed two more features, 30 Minutes Or Less, and Gangster Squad.

It was really his website which inspired me to test the 'apprentice' water. His blog posts made me want to work in film. So I ambitiously fired off email after email. Emails to the offices of Spielberg, Lucas, Scorsese - name them and they probably got one. I don't have access to it anymore, but one of those emails was to Ruben and it probably featured something now very cringeworthy which only an overly enthusiastic 18 year old can write, like:

"Huge fan and follow your blog and read every post. Just wondered if you were in need of an assistant on any of your future work? It would be awesome to help."

Anyone who mentions the obvious facts that I was 17, lived on a different continent and wasn't eligible for a visa is a dream-crusher. Screw you, dream crushers.

A few days later, there was a reply along the lines of:

"Sorry man but I'm not looking for an assistant at the moment. Plus, if anything comes up I'd probably be wise to choose someone a bit more local. Thanks though!"

Not surprisingly, nothing came of those email blasts, but for the next few years I kept checking in on the blog. In between posts about new work, there'd be updates about road biking and travelling, so when the wheels started to turn on this bike-based people project, he was an obvious person to meet. But making it too obvious that someone has been influential can come off as weird, so despite being a little nervous, I tried to forget all that.

The shoot was for a pilot episode of a new show about witness protection, and today the schedule would have the crew film some second-unit scenes and then blow up a van.

Maybe it was just me being a bit of a production nerd, but I was excited and there was an electricity in the air. In retrospect, it must have been self-created energy because the lighting guy didn't seem as fired up as he sat by a grip truck and chain-smoked. I suppose there's a lesson in that - when you become used to anything, the magic can fade. Depending on the day, similar feelings had tainted my view of cycling.

As I set up the interview gear with Samira, over walked Ruben, fresh off filming a scene. He was inquisitive, asked where the bike was, and wanted to talk about riding.

The juxtaposition was obvious and amusing. To record the interview, I had a single backpack with a small camera and a cheap microphone in it, and a makeshift approach which involved balancing the microphone precariously. Yet here we were on a filmset with cranes and trucks and lighting rigs literally worth millions of dollars. The on-set sound recordist probably didn't balance his mic on his rucksack.

At the start of his career, Ruben's approach had been low-scale. "I was 26 when I was like, finally, yeah that's what I wanna do, and that's when I shot my short film. Now I'm 38 so I guess it's been 12 years, trying to get to where I'm at."

His first project involved a single camera and an idea to make a documentary about Chicago musicians. "I bought a video camera and I decided I wanted to make a documentary. I'd never shot anything before that."

"It wasn't much different than this," he laughed, looking at the microphone, tentatively swaying in the breeze.

Without any connections or a background in film, he had resorted to guerrilla tactics to get people in his documentary.

"I flew to Chicago, and literally didn't know any of them, so I went to a record store and got the phone number off the record and called the record people and was like 'Hi I'm making a documentary about Ghetto Tracks, can I talk to you about it? So I just kind of barged my way in to these dudes homes," he chuckled.

There were some parallels in our approach, if you swap the phone calls with a few emails.

We can learn a lot from another person's story - their struggles and successes and doubts - so I asked Ruben about what the 12 year path had been like. The typical route to filmmaking, for a long time, was go to film school and network, so a story of someone carving out their own path in this industry, without doing that, is unique.

"There's friends I can think of that were way funnier than me, or way more talented," he said. "And I think they were afraid to take the risk. Whereas for me, the one talent I think I have, more than anything else, is persistence. I just won't give up. And so when I was trying to be a director, I put myself $35,000 in debt trying to do that, but I was determined that it was going to work out. I wasn't going to stop until I'd figured it out. It just was unfathomable."

"Once I said, 'I'm going to start directing', and I just stopped working for other people, and shot short films and low-budget music videos, that's when nothing was handed to me. I just kept on shooting, shooting, shooting, shooting, and then gradually people started to pay attention, and then it kept just growing very organically. And it has, because it's been almost 10 years now, starting from a $50 music video, to features for studios."

In many stories, there is often a dirty start, where the reality is miles away from the idealism of the destination. A period where, like riding a bike for a fucking long time, you think that it's never going to work out and want to stop. I asked Ruben about whether he'd been through that.

"I was broke and bummed and frustrated, and so ambitious," he spoke intensely. "But it doesn't happen overnight. So many people that were more veteran than me were just like 'dude, cherish these moments, because it's never gonna be like this again, and you're doing cool shit, and appreciate everything that you're doing in the moment, because whether you make it or not, you're doing it. You're trying, you're having fun, you're making stuff that you believe in, cherish it. Try not to get so caught up on the future and just appreciate the present. And that's a really hard thing to say when you're so focused on the destination, but it was great advice. I probably didn't take it, at all, but now I look back on those times of finding it and the struggle so fondly, because it was real and personal..."

There was definitely a selfish aspect to the reasons behind these questions - I wanted to know if any lessons from another persons story could be applied to my own. I think Ruben recognised the root of the questioning.

"...So I would say, if I was cycling 12,000 miles across a country talking to people I'd never met before, I can't imagine a cooler project. And no matter what happens with any of this, the experience in and of itself should be the thing to really cherish."

Those insights would be valuable to refer to when confidence was low.

And oh, the explosion - can't finish this chapter without talking about the explosion. It was massive. The truck was blown to smithereens. It was very exciting, and funnily enough, wouldn't have been out of place at Camp Pendleton.

We all start off as beginners, we all struggle, we all have doubts and problems, there is always a dirty start, and if we want to get somewhere, we often have to stay in the game long enough to see it through.

Yet maybe getting somewhere isn't the most important part. Even though the journey might seem like a slow one at times, if we're doing stuff that we know we should be doing, and moving in the right direction, then just being on the path ought to be reason enough.

To be honest, for much of the time whilst riding around North America, the real meaning of 'why' was unclear, and it wasn't obvious whether it would lead to anything after all was said and done. But deep down, it did feel like the right place to be. Trusting that to be the case was never easy, but after this day, whenever doubts on the road or a lack of confidence occurred, "Cherish it" is the message that I tried to remember.

Riding away from the set, I was happy. The initial skepticism, caused by the dick in the Range Rover, was long gone. In any place, you get jerks, but as was a constant theme throughout the journey, mostly you get open and helpful people.

18

Prison And
Passing It On

STINSON BEACH IS 23 MILES AWAY FROM SAN FRANCISCO. To get there, you cross Golden Gate Bridge and are soon greeted with some of the most spectacular landscapes imaginable in Marin County, California's infamous wine country. There's green rolling hills, with inclines all brutal on the legs, plus forest and the incredible rocky, dramatic and wave-heavy Pacific.

Cycling into the small beach town late at night, I quickly set up camp in the local state park near the beach.

At 5:45 A.M., a blurry figure that I couldn't make out was kicking the canvas a few inches away from my face. A unique alarm clock, apparently without a snooze or shut-the-hell-up button. The mysterious figure turned out to be a park ranger, doing the rounds as part of his morning duties.

"Get Up! Get Up! You've got 5 minutes! You'd better be out of here when I get back!" he demanded, fiercely.

In all honesty, this kind of situation wasn't rare, and had happened a few times in a variety of state parks along the way. Life strapped to a set of wheels forces you to become fairly adept when it comes to sleeping. Unfortunately, a side-effect of this is often operating in a half-zombie state of compounded tiredness.

So despite the initial shock of the wake up call, it was business as usual. Wake up, pack up, warm up and move on. That is the bike-life routine.

For once I wasn't alone in this, though. Someone else was having a similar morning. Yawning, and rubbing his eyes from a lack of quality sleep, a figure that had been sleeping on the beach, less than a hundred metres away, stumbled by.

He was Bradford 'Brad' Haith, on the way to get his usual morning coffee. It was on his return, whilst I tried to stuff my tent into the pannier bag, that we spoke properly. His story was entirely out of the blue. Brad described how he had ended up in jail.

"When I went in, I was 14 years old," he recalled in a faded East Coast accent. "It was originally for selling drugs, and I got busted. Which is OK, I felt, because I was doing bad. They was gonna charge me with a distribution charge, but I was using, you know? So I just told them 'OK, I'm using', and they gave me a lesser charge, which was 24 months."

Brad grew up in Boston. When he was caught selling and using drugs, he was locked up for two years.

"I did 18 months out of this," he continued, "and inside the jail I was in 'the hole'. You have 23 hour lockdown, and I was there for 6 months out of the 18 months. In this isolation place, they wasn't treating us very respectfully, or just good, at all. So it just came to a point and one day they let us out for the hour, and I got frustrated. They came to me. They asked me to go back to my cell and I didn't. And so they came in to get me, 8 guards, and I didn't wanna go back, so I hit 2 of them. And they gave me 8 years for that."

That incident increased his sentence to a decade behind bars. It was shocking to think that a blip, made out of frustration on a single day in a single moment, could add another 8 years to someone's jail sentence.

Without anything else to do, for the remaining 102 months, he decided to try and keep his head down and get through it. He succeeded in making it to the end, and was eventually released.

When he told me what happened on release day, I couldn't believe it. I'd just assumed that there must be some kind of readjustment process in place for inmates who've done long stretches.

"They gave me a sixty dollar check, and a piece of paper with my photograph, to go to the bank and cash the check after 10 years," Brad said, almost jovially, until recalling his mindset at the time.

"They dropped me off right downtown Boston. Thousands of people. I didn't understand what... who... I was taken care of for 10 years. I didn't know how to live, you know? But I was scared and nervous, because I didn't know how to react around all these people or nothing. So I seen a crossing guard, across the street, and I said 'well, if I go hit this guy, I can go right back home.' But my emotions inside me said 'no, just give it some time.'"

To tell you a bit more about Brad, he's tall, around 40, carries a rucksack around all the time, and was just immediately upbeat and positive, beaming with life, despite being homeless and finding that hard going at times. He's a guy who embraces the world at 6am through tired eyes, which is rare.

It's easy to imagine that you could go through something like 10 years in prison and become jaded with the world, but he wasn't.

Shocking enough as his story of imprisonment had been, it was the next chapter of his life, the part where he did something to actively change his life, that was the most remarkable.

"When I got out in 1999, I decided to change my life," he recalled proudly. "So I grabbed a bag, and I wanted to help people. I always loved helping people. So I decided to walk, and give out the energy that I had that was holding inside of me. I wasn't sure if this was good energy, positive energy... I was a little upset when I got out too. Because it was like, 'what am I to do now', you know? I had a small backpack, and no food or anything. I just wanted to give out some good energy and break away, like a release, from where I was, and travel. It changed my life. I shook every hand I could shake, and met everyone from just about every nationality."

He walked.

"From Boston, I walked up to Vermont. I started the Appalachian trail. That took me like 3 months, 4 months. I decided at that time to go to a place I'd not been before. I walked back to Boston, and from Boston I went to Florida, and that took over a year. I met a cyclist, who had cycled from California, to Florida where we had met. And I thought, 'How interesting. If he can cycle, I could possibly walk."

He kept walking.

"All in all, I think I did 37 or 38 states. Across the country twice. All of Florida. All of California. And all of the East Coast. After 13 years, I stopped 6 months ago. I love this place."

Brad had quite literally walked away from a negative past to carve out a different future. He had walked for even longer than the decade he'd been imprisoned. He talked about some of the most adventurous moments I've ever heard of, which had happened to him over the last 13 years. Snake attacks. Bears. Losing everything. The fight to stay away from a place that brought back painful memories and painful habits.

Brad survived on odd bits of work, dumpster diving and generous handouts. I asked him about whether he got frustrated living like a nomad, because I certainly did at times. He quickly knocked down any such concept.

"Look at where we're at!" he exclaimed. "The biggest house in the world, is the world. With no bills! The sun is rising right now. That's my heater. When it goes down, I turn on the AC, and the AC comes on. I don't have to pay no bills. This is as natural as you get it. It's simplistic."

That reply, I think, shows a couple of things. One is how awesome the planet can be, and how we probably don't appreciate it enough, and another is an underlying strength and resilience within Brad that is motivating and should inspire action when times seem dark. He seemed truly happy.

As is often the case, whenever someone was willing to talk about a sensitive topic, a connection was made. It seemed like a bond had been created between Brad and I, and we played basketball for the rest of the morning.

He talked about how hard it was trying to find food sometimes, but how content he was to experience nature every day. He talked about the moments on the road that have caused fear, anger, and joy. His life was full of these incredible, insane stories - terrible and amazing - and he'd accumulated so much experience about overcoming hardship.

I wondered what he wanted to do now he'd stopped walking, and he spoke about a desire to talk to kids who might be able to learn from his stories.

"I think passing it on is important, because once I have received what I have received, it's not fair for me to hold it in for myself. I think it's good to share it. My childhood was in jail. Prison. Penitentiary. And it was tougher, rougher. I didn't have a life. This is why I believe in positive energy, and good natured people. Because when you do something good, it comes back. It's the cycle of life, I believe."

Stories have the power to move us all, and to change us, and Brad's was as incredible as they come. He'd walked away when it was easier to walk back inside.

19

No Such Thing As A Free Lunch

Iᴛ ᴡᴀs ᴀ ʙᴇᴀᴜᴛɪꜰᴜʟ ɴɪɢʜᴛ. Tʜᴇ sᴋʏ ᴡᴀs ᴄʟᴇᴀʀ ᴀɴᴅ ᴅᴀʀᴋ, the stars shining and fully on display. Too good to be true, perhaps?

The park was cold, but it looked vivid and remarkably green, as though it was really taken care of.

It was late when I settled on the idea of sleeping there. Maybe it was a lack of motivation and psyche, but finding somewhere more suitable just didn't happen. I looked and looked but it seemed like a better place than anywhere else. So I began the usual routine of unloading sleeping bag, bivy bag, stuff-sack full of clothes to act as a pillow, roll mat. Those things in unison provided at least a little bit of home comfort. There was no need for a tent tonight. There was no rain, so a bivy under the stars seemed much more appealing, plus it was faster to set up.

The little fuckers were set on a timer.

They had been invisible for the first couple of hours as I lay on the park bench in my bivy bag. No wonder the grass was so bloody vivid - high-pressure sprinklers were automatically switched on at night.

Small metal sprayers rose out of the ground like something from Thunderbirds and began to fire off freezing streams of water, rotating to soak literally everything in sight. I became drenched within seconds. PSSSSTTT. That's the sound the water from the sprinkler would make as it hit the bench and everything in proximity.

I got up, walked to the car park, and angrily dumped everything down on the gravel. The soaking gear, wet down sleeping bag and cold temperature resulted in one of the worst nights sleep I'd ever had.

It was April, and time was running out. My second visa in the US expired at the beginning of May, and that meant attempting to cover 980 miles - the rest of California, plus Oregon and Washington - in under three weeks.

Up to that point, ignoring a car-only bridge with Jermaine Daniels, a short ferry crossing when the land ran out, and a very brief mechanical-fix ride near Santa Cruz with a kind local driver called Michael, forward progress on the journey had been human-powered since setting out. However, it was becoming more and more obvious, from looking at my previous daily average, that there was little chance reaching Canada exclusively using pedal strokes would work.

Ignoring that though, I rode on, reasoning that whatever happens happens. And shortly thereafter I arrived in a town called Gualala.

The town is a small 2,000 person community, 95 miles North of Stinson Beach. And like every other conversation, it started innocently.

"Woah! Where are you going?" he shouted.

He introduced himself as Charlie, and we spoke for a few minutes. I didn't ask his age but a guesstimate would put him around 65. He had recently moved to Gualala from San Francisco, and had retired from banking. He was looking to purchase the derelict hotel that we were stood outside of.

We spoke about travelling and road life and the state of San Francisco and how it's changed in the last 5 years. "It used to be the best place on earth, my friend, the best place on earth!" Charlie shouted.

Then he abruptly asked my age, and that was really the turning point of the day.

"How old are you anyway, to be doing this? Don't you have a wife and kids back home?"

"No, no wife or kids," I said. "I'm 23. Actually, sorry... I just turned 24, like two days ago."

"So it's your birthday? Did you celebrate?"

"Is being on the road kind of celebrating?"

"Shut up!" he joked. "I mean did you actually celebrate, with drinks and dinner?"

"No, not really."

"Right. I'm making a call to Chris," he said, assuming that every other human knew who Chris was. "We're going to a restaurant. I'm buying you lunch, whatever you want. We're going to celebrate your birthday."

Undeniably, an awesomely kind thing to do.

We agreed to meet a couple of hours later at a restaurant at the other side of town. The 'other side of town' only meant a few hundred metres, but Charlie had to rush home for something.

It wasn't clear if this was a legitimate offer, so I half-expected to show up to a posh restaurant and find nobody there, followed by making an awkward retreat, mumbling an apology about being in the wrong place.

Surprisingly, though, Charlie was sat there along with the Chris that he'd called on the phone earlier. Both of them were in tuxedo's, which was quite a stark contrast to the typical bicycle traveller's attire.

Chris was younger than Charlie, maybe 40. They didn't look dissimilar so I thought maybe they were father and son.

The moment I realised that Charlie and Chris were lovers was about 1 minute into the conversation when Chris mentioned he was married to a man back in San Francisco but it's an open relationship and he sees Charlie 4 days each week.

We ordered. I saw fish and chips on the menu and jumped straight for that. A bit of home comfort, y'know? They both got lobster and Charlie finished the order by requesting a bottle of local wine.

It was overwhelmingly upmarket, and like the soon to be eaten battered cod, I felt like a fish out of water in these grand surroundings. There were chandeliers hanging, and an ocean view on display. So far, so good. It was all very nice, and a much appreciated break from the saddle or the tent which were normality.

The food arrived and it was incredible. But the conversation grew stranger by the minute, as we moved through two courses.

Charlie went on a couple of rants about the state of the government and how he thinks the FBI has been following him for years because he's so "edgy" and "a revolutionary." It was hard to figure out why he thought this, so I quizzed him on how this had come about, and his answers were just more and more confusing, about "the establishment" and how he was a "valuable target" because of his trading background. It didn't make any sense at all, but he wouldn't talk about the backstory.

Charlie was definitely the outspoken one of the couple. Chris was mostly sat quietly just nodding along with everything Charlie said. It seemed almost like he didn't dare offend Charlie. Because he was so edgy and revolutionary probably.

"What's the deal with the open relationship and your marriage then, Chris?" I asked in an attempt to get him to open up. Might as well be blunt.

"His marriage doesn't mean shit," Charlie jumped in, for all to hear. "He's going to get a divorce and move in with me. We just bought a $650,000 house together just a few days ago."

Money was clearly one of the most important things to Charlie, and he relished the opportunity to tell anyone about it.

"It's a really nice place, right by the ocean," Chris admitted shyly, in contrast.

"We were just there actually... having a bit of afternoon fun...," as Charlie said this, he demonstrated what he meant by 'afternoon fun' by making a circle with his thumb and index finger on one hand, and then inserting his middle finger from his other hand into this circle repeatedly, whilst making slurping noises.

In and out. Slurp. In and out.

"You know what they say," Charlie said with a hint of slyness, "there ain't no such thing as a free lunch... We're going to go back to our place to keep on drinking. You look tired, and there's plenty of room. It's a beautiful day, you should come relax with us, not ride your bike. We were talking... we want you to join us in a pleasure session."

It had been memorable, but it was clear we wouldn't stay in touch. We parted ways uncomfortably.

20

Breaking The
Cycle

Avenue of the Giants is truly wonderful. It's a 32 mile stretch of the most idyllic road imaginable, which runs parallel to U.S. Route 101 through Humboldt Redwoods State Park.

In April, it was quiet, beautiful, and out-of-season, so it seemed like a hidden paradise that had managed to avoid detection by the masses. The subtle road that tracked through the redwoods provided everything a landscape needs in order to induce a childlike sense of wonder and fascination with nature.

In the air, drifted a perfect euphoric pine smell. Without traffic, empty, it was possible to play games on the road, slaloming in-between the yellow lines whilst looking up at the trees which stretched upwards towards the roof of the world.

Usually, the Avenue draws crowds, especially in the summer. People flock to take photos under the Drive-Through Tree in the tiny town of Leggett, or the Immortal Tree, a redwood which has been standing for an estimated 950 years despite floods and direct lighting strikes. They come to swim in the vast gorges and beautiful beaches of Eel River. This place has it all, and it was one of the most stunning places that I'd ever cycled through.

The only interaction I had in the Avenue of the Giants was a 30 second conversation with Maggie, a retired teacher who was spending months in an enormous RV with her husband. She came over, saw me downing an ungodly amount of Dr Pepper outside of a tiny gas station, and simply said "you look tired," before explaining what her road trip plans were and quickly getting in her RV and driving South. She was right.

Pedalling lightly, in a low gear for hours and hours, I stopped frequently to just sit and take in the soaring redwoods. Riding surrounded by the Giants, it was one of those great periods where troubles and worries fizzled away. Nature's beauty has a big and often unconscious impact on your mood, lifting you from darkness. Those kind of times were my favourite.

Waking up in the tent the following day, now in the small city of Fortuna and with bleary eyes, I unzipped the canvas and looked out from a makeshift camp site overlooking Eel river.

It was decision time. As expected, it was now pretty obvious that cycling to the Canada border was not going to happen within the limits of the visa deadline.

But there was a Greyhound bus.

In two days it departed from Eureka, a city just 17 miles ahead, and went all the way up to Seattle, close to the border. That meant skipping 585 miles, but it also essentially meant guaranteeing crossing the border on time.

Choosing to book a bus ticket might sound like an non-decision. It's just a bloody bus ticket after all. But at the time the decision was a stressful one. Was it admitting defeat?

That question seems completely irrelevant and stupid now, but I had worked it up in my mind and, from the trenches, lacked perspective, so it was a hard decision to make. I guess, despite a now very low daily average with the occasional big day thrown in when motivation struck, I was still oddly tied to the trip having some aspect of athleticism to it. It felt like getting the bus would be like throwing in the towel.

In Eureka, it became clear that the rear wheel - the same one that had been replaced months ago after off-roading in Alabama - was finally starting to give up. Two spokes had snapped and were now rattling around. Luckily they were on the non-drive side, so were easy enough to replace. You couldn't complain really, though. Since Alabama, the wheel had been completely forgotten about. But at some point, good luck has to end, and looking back now, that day in Eureka was the beginning of a period of consistent mechanical trouble.

The Greyhound bus journey went via a confusing route, which meant taking a big step back before moving forwards. From Eureka, there were then three transfers. One at Oakland, 275 miles South along the same roads I had used to get here. Another at Sacramento. And the last one at Portland, Oregon, before the final journey to Seattle.

There were 5 other people waiting at the hard-to-find bus shelter on a small street in Eureka. It was due to arrive at 7AM. When the enormous, silver bus pulled in, the driver got off to help everyone on. Everyone had pre-booked and almost all were travelling lightly, so just stepped on with a single rucksack or suitcase and found their seat.

The first driver was great. He saw the bike, opened the luggage compartment, and said that "even though it should have tags and be in a box, there's plenty of room so just slide it in. You just need to pick up tags when we get to Oakland." So I lifted the bike in, and placed the pannier bags within the frame triangle to avoid them slipping around.

We arrived in Oakland hours later and the journey had seemingly gotten off to a great start, without any hitches. At the all-day transfer, the receptionist behind the travel desk was standoffish. Serving Greyhound customers obviously wasn't a personal passion. She scanned my ticket and printed out some elasticated paper tags to attach to the bike.

"You really need to put it in a box too. It's policy," she said flippantly.

Everything would've gone a lot smoother had I realised this policy and picked up a box from a bike shop.

"Oh right. Um. I don't have one. Sorry. Anything you can do?"

She told me to wait whilst she went to talk to the driver, and after five minutes she came back and said, "it's okay, you're lucky because there's room in the luggage compartment. Just make sure you put tags on all the loose bags. I'll print more off for you now." She even smiled a little bit when she said this, which was surprising. She was willing to flex the rules, the antithesis of a Jobsworth.

Back on Greyhound, it was a short two hour journey to Sacramento. We set off at 9pm and it was going well. The bus was sweaty and cramped, but we were getting somewhere and only bellends complain about legroom. The passing towns, lit up in the night and glowing tungsten, were novel because life at speeds faster than 10 miles per hour were unusual these days.

The next transfer, at the bus station in Sacramento at 11pm, was when everything took a turn for the worst.

"There's no way you're putting that dirty bike on the bus. It's policy. You have to have a box," the young Sacramento bus station worker said, bluntly with a hint of anger, and a twinge of someone who loves making other peoples lives difficult. I don't know his name but it was potentially Jeremy Jobsworth.

"Oh the Greyhound lady at Oakland said there was room so it should be okay," I said without thinking too much about it.

"No. Did I not just tell you?! Are you deaf? You have to have a box!" He squawked, like a really annoying crow. The dude had got out of bed on the wrong side.

I really hate dealing with people who like power and aren't willing to bend corporation policy even a bit. When someone gets verbally angry for no reason, I find it hard not to retaliate with more verbal anger. It's a problem. So I snapped back "do you like being so unhelpful?" and walked off.

In the depths of the Greyhound website, it talks about bike boxes. So the guy was right, and another lapse in research seemed to be taking it's revenge. I went back fifteen minutes later, calmer and attempting to be more rational.

"The bus sets off in an hour. I don't have a box. Sorry but I don't. I know that it's policy. Unless you can point me in the direction of somewhere that sells massive boxes, then do you have any other suggestions that could help? Because at the moment, I have a ticket for that bus and only that bus, and I want to make sure I'm on it."

"We have bike boxes but there's no way yours is going to fit in it. You can try, but it won't fit and excess baggage fees will cost you $40."

"Can I see the box?"

"Yeah, here it is."

He brought a tiny box out of the back. It seemed unlikely, but maybe poking some holes in it and dismantling most of the bike would mean it would at least sit in the box and might be enough for them to let it pass.

The final question was a cheeky one, but it was truthful. The trip was taking longer than expected, and my bank balance was getting slimmer. Every dollar counted, so throwing $40 down on a cardboard box and excess charges for one bus journey seemed absurd.

"I don't have $40. Can you do...?"

"Listen man," Jeremy shouted, "I've told you and told you. Do you want me to pull some fucking dollars out of my ass?"

"You're an unhelpful dickhead," I snapped again.

Pissed off and seeing more red than I had done in a long time, I left, now adamantly ready to attempt to stash the bike on the bus without Jeremy Jobsworth seeing. And if he did, then I was increasingly willing to participate in a fight to the death.

There was another Greyhound staff member, stood behind Jeremy, and she had heard what essentially was the childish shouting match between us. She walked over and said, "he can't actually do that."

"What can't he do?"

I guess Greyhound have a fear of complaints about staff, so if a staff member swears at a customer they basically will do anything to make it right. Even if the passenger swears back. There's the leverage, baby.

The woman was much kinder. She calmed me down and brought a box out, and apologised for her colleague.

Just as guilty as Jeremy, if not way more so, I thanked her, and when the bus arrived, loaded the bike into the luggage compartment. In the reserved seat by the window, as we pulled out I made eye contact with Jeremy, staring at him with mean glee, a glow of petty success. It wasn't a proud moment, but seeing the anger boil up in his face did feel great.

The next bus leg was a long stretch through the night. The cabin was half-full when we set off, but became fuller with each stop made at small towns along the way.

An old man got on. He had silver hair, a rugged beard, worn boots and a torn coat, and smelt of stale beer. He looked like he'd seen a lot of things in his life. He walked to find his seat.

Whilst everyone else tried to grab some shuteye in the early hours, he delved into his black leather rucksack and opened up a pornographic magazine which he thoroughly and proudly read for a good hour to pass the time.

Occasionally people would wake up and see the pages, and small gasps could be heard coming from nearby rows. This was his own magazine-based version of a pleasure session.

21

An Entrepreneur
And A Crossing

As I walked through the gritty streets of Seattle, a thought nagged at the front of my mind. I wondered whether 'giving in' and taking motorised transport now meant it would become an accepted norm in the harder times. Hopefully not, but the simple act of stepping on that bus in Eureka meant the bike-all-the-way mentality was dented.

But, everything was back on track, visa deadlines no longer concerning.

Being in any big city was tricky, especially living the rough camping life. Looking after the bike when not riding it, sometimes caused me to feel resentment to the whole 'fun travel' thing. When you just want to enjoy a place in a regular way and walk around, the bike can be a metaphorical set of handcuffs. You take it everywhere, or you constantly worry about it.

There's also another self-conscious factor that might seem irrational but still caused issues. When you walk around with a bicycle that has huge bags strapped to it, and are dirty and worn down, people judge you. The glances and strange looks of the people who see a sweaty, dirty traveller, begin to nag and cause anxiety.

In towns and rural places, people were mostly excited about seeing something unusual. Greetings were joyous and easy. But in cities, people often assumed you were a weirdo or a hobo, and would go out of their way to avoid you. That single aspect had the power to be the most disheartening of all.

WarmShowers.org is a website that enables cycle tourists to find a host willing to provide a couch or bed for the night, and when they've finished their trip, it allows them to register as a host and reciprocate the favour. It is a very cool tool, and when you're feeling like the staring eyes are becoming a bit much, it can be a good service to utilise in order to get clean, rested, and feel normal again.

There were a couple of gripes with it though. One was that it can complicate your days. When you're moving at your own pace, you get into this self-supported way of just going about each day. There are no real worries other than finding somewhere to sleep each night. A small price you pay when using WarmShowers can be a pressure to be somewhere by a certain time.

The other reason I struggled with using it frequently, was because you inevitably end up talking about bicycles all the time. Some of my WarmShowers experiences had been amazing, but others were quite hard work, involving strained conversations about handlebar specs, cogs and gear ratios. That happened three times consecutively, so I'd taken a break.

But then I spent a couple of days camping in the pouring rain, in the woods outside Seattle, and started to experience intense cabin fever, so figured maybe it was worth another punt. No-one likes to be sleepless in Seattle. I logged on and sent some requests for hosts in the area.

Emily and John, a couple who lived in the suburbs of the city, replied almost instantly and said they had a couch that any fellow bicycle traveller was welcome to. For a long time, I found it a bit mind-blowing when people who you've never met are willing to go out of their way to help. Anyone who's travelled long-term must've experience it too - an immense sense of gratitude towards anyone willing to help. I am indebted to a lot of people like Emily and John.

Emily was a freelance designer with an imminent deadline and wasn't at home much during the two nights, but the first night we clinked glasses filled with homemade mojitos and ate a salmon dinner. Oh, that's another thing that's awesome about staying with hosts - homemade food that's not pasta or noodles or banana sandwiches.

John was around during the day. He worked from home, and was the founder of a bicycle gear and apparel company called 'High Above Designs', making high quality outdoor bags.

Their house was a great place to rest. The ability to leave the bike and walk around the city on foot was bliss. But one of my favourite moments in Seattle had nothing to do with the place itself, and instead involved the chance to chat to John about starting his company. We spoke in his workshop, amongst fabric, widgets and sewing machines, where he made the bespoke items each day.

Leaving the production business, back in Manchester, had knocked my confidence for all things entrepreneurial, but John was making it work. He was an entrepreneur living it, in the trenches, not burned out, and speaking to him stoked a fire in my belly that had been dim for some time.

He was in his late twenties, in a hoody and jeans and clearly his own boss, and he talked about how he had ended up creating his company, which was going from strength to strength.

"I'm coming up on 2 years since I got fired from my last job," he smiled. "A good friend had a ski company and was thinking about making a pack. He said to me, whilst I was still working at my former business, 'I need a prototype made.' And I agreed to do it, and I also prefaced it with him that I really didn't know what I was doing. He was like, 'that's OK, you can learn' and from his entrepreneurial standpoint it was; what you need to know, you will learn."

"So he gave me this project, and right as that project started I was fired from my last job for bringing my dog into work," he said with a tint of bitterness, as his dog Wizard lay relaxed on the carpet. "I remember calling him and being like 'Dan, I'm so screwed. I don't have a sewing machine to use anymore'. He said 'You should go get one.' And I remember thinking - that's so simple. His entrepreneurial spirit was saying 'there's nothing that stops you, there are things that slow you down, and it's the way you deal with them and the way you move past them'. And that was an eye-opener for me, because self-employment didn't really seem viable. And now I realise that there's no other way... there's no other way."

I asked John about how someone knows when it's time to go it alone. How can you tell when a good time to make the jump is? Why lose security to risk trying something that might not work?

"If you're in a job that doesn't pay what you want, and doesn't give you the satisfaction you want... or it does, and the people that you're working for don't appreciate that... For the people that dump their heart into their work, and their boss doesn't see it or doesn't care... I would highly recommend to those people, entrepreneurship. I'd highly recommend it."

John had found the thing for him, he'd worked hard for it and it was starting to gain traction. I think that's a good lesson in dedication, motivation and self-belief.

When Emily came back in the evening, I was packing up the bike in preparation to leave the city the next day. She asked about which route I was going to take to get to Canada.

"I guess I'll just keep heading up the coast," I said, dumbly.

"Oh, what? You can't do that," she said excitedly. "You should go up Puget Sound and take the San Juan Islands!"

The San Juan Islands are an archipelago in between the mainland US and Vancouver Island, Canada. With a bit of planning, you can hop on some cheap ferries, ride the islands, and work your way up to Canada. I was completely oblivious to this island range until Emily mentioned it, so I didn't really grasp the reason behind taking this route.

"They're regularly voted one of the most beautiful places in the world," she jumped in to explain. "Seriously, just riding from here up the mainland will suck and you'll be in built up areas most of the way. Take the ferries between the islands and ride from port to port."

The next day I set off to the port, waved goodbye to Seattle and boarded the first of several ferries to Bainbridge Island.

On the islands, I was reminded of how the way we frame situations in our minds can make such a big difference to the way we perceive them. Stealth camping on the islands wasn't a chore, it was a luxury. There was no need for a tent, so I bivyed overlooking the water, on a shingly beach just metres away from Puget Sound.

There was no-one around, it was deserted, yet the Seattle skyline was just across the water, where the Space Needle towered and the distant lights indicated a city which is always on. In the background, the water lapped along the rocks and created a relaxing metronome. There was no self-consciousness, paranoia or anxiety here.

And only a couple of days ago I'd been fucking hating stealth camping. Everything is about perspective.

I rode and rode, then took short ferry trips, then rode and rode some more. The island roads were deserted, they were perfect. And because I'd skipped a state by taking the bus, the landscape was completely new, and hadn't become naturally dulled in my mind, so the days were good.

At 1PM on May 5th, the inky passport stamp hit the page, and the guard said "Welcome To Canada."

22

A Reputation Of Mountains

THE FREQUENT PING NOISE AND THE SUDDEN JOLT FEELING made it obvious without even having to look down to confirm. Spokes were snapping every day and it was getting really annoying.

There is a stretch of British Columbia - from Vancouver through the mountains, past Squamish and Whistler - where you have the bustling city nestled on the coast, and a short distance away you have huge mountains. It has to be one of the best places on the planet to be if you've an interest in living an outdoor lifestyle. You can tick the city-living, surfing, climbing, river and snow boxes at the same time.

The geographic spectacle of British Columbia wasn't enough to stop the frustrations that come with riding a bike with a wheel that was falling apart spoke by spoke though.

Whistler is a worldwide mountain bikers mecca, particularly in the summer when the ski lifts are used to take adrenalin-filled bikers to the top of the now snow-free slopes before they ride as fast as possible down them. It's a buzzing place, and conveniently, there's a wealth of experienced mechanics and bike shops in town, so if there was ever a good place to sort a wheel out, it was here.

Every shop was set up for mountain bikes with smaller wheels, and no-one had anything in stock. All of them were happy to order in a new wheel, but said that it would take two weeks to arrive. One of the mechanics at Whistler Bike Co. looked at the wheel and suggested that I should just carry a lot more spokes and replace them each time another one snapped. It wouldn't be a long-term fix but it might be enough to continue rolling on whilst organising another wheel to get sent to a post office ahead.

Looking at the map, it looked like, as long as the order was placed in the next few days, there would be time to get a wheel sent to Prince George, under 400 miles away, and have it waiting there on arrival. So for now, I zip-tied a handful of spokes to the bike, 20 or so, and carried on up the coast along the Sea-to-Sky Highway, attempting to ignore the increasingly less round, weak and battered wheel.

Later that evening, I rode into Pemberton, a town North of Whistler. There was a fast-food joint attached to the gas station and it did a stellar milkshake. Two policemen walked in. This might be a massive generalisation, but Canadian police officers seem quite un-intimidating in comparison to other countries.

"Is that your bike outside?" Steve the policeman asked.

If you are reading this and struggle to initiate conversations, get a bike and stick some bags on it. It won't take you more than half an hour to find yourself involved in some sort of deep chat.

Steve reeled off his bucket list and spoke about how he wants to get back to his Scottish and Irish roots and go on a motorcycle tour around Europe. Maybe many of us are struck with a 'grass is always greener' mentality, because almost every American and Canadian I met who dreamt of long-distance travel wanted to escape to Europe or Asia, and almost every other long-distance cyclist I bumped into on this continent was from a different part of the world.

Steve confirmed that camping anywhere in British Columbia is fine and legal as long as it's not private property. That was a huge weight lifted because it meant sleeping by the side of the road was actually okay, and there was no, when preparing camp, to spend a long time attempting to avoid detection.

"Why, is that where you're sleeping tonight? By the side of the road?" Steve asked with a hint of concern.

"Probably now that you've just said it's legal! Know anywhere good?"

"I'm pretty sure I can trust you. And hopefully because you can see I'm a police officer you trust that I'm not a serial killer either. I have a basement where I keep my bikes and it has a pull-out bed. You can stay there if you want? I have to work until 4 in the morning. You can have the basement and use the kitchen if you want. Beats camping, doesn't it?"

Something about the word basement threw me off initially. A couple of days earlier, three women from Ohio had been found after being kidnapped, and then being held captive and abused for more than ten years. On hearing the news, I wondered whether the 'everyone is friendly' approach might be naive. But this dude was a cop.

"That would be amazing."

The next day I woke up, dead.

Just kidding, I was fully rested, not tied up, and still alive. No surprises there then. Steve was up early, despite finishing the night shift at ridiculous o'clock. He cooked a huge breakfast, accompanied by the best maple syrup I've ever tasted, and he spoke about something that had become increasingly topical.

Just the day prior, a mechanic in Whistler had said "It's probably going to be the worst hill of the whole thing." He was talking about the Pemberton 'mountain'.

Mount Currie. A mountain ascent with, easily, the fiercest reputation that I'd ever come across. And the climb wasn't just famous for the steepness or the length, it also had a reputation for what was waiting at the top.

Leaving Steve's place, I freewheeled into town and bumped into some British expats who ran a pizza truck.

Simon and Carol had escaped the city in London in search of a more relaxed, outdoor life and had ended up here. It must've been only half an hour between eating breakfast and then moving on to pizza. But screw it, a man needs his energy if he's about to climb the toughest mountain in the world...

As we sat outside the pizza van, chatting about The Tube and Simon and Carol's previous career burnouts that led them here, a French paraglider came to get a pizza. He saw the bike, and immediately broke into a speech that would have Keanu Reeves shivering in his boots.

"Oh man. You're going over Currie on a bike? Killer... There's tons of moose and bear up there... My granddad was chased by a moose once. He ran up a tree and the moose waited at the bottom for two days before it got bored... And be careful of cougars too. They hide in trees and jump out at humans... And there's wolves that hunt in packs..."

You quickly learn to try to ignore these reputations, but this hill came with so much chatter, it became much more intimidating than the rest.

I started to climb Mount Currie with the same drill I'd used on all the other mountains up to this point. Granny ring. One stroke after another. Get in a rhythm. Put your head down. Become lost in thought. Ignore the loose and rattling spokes.

It was working. Thoughts of killer animals faded and the surroundings became inspiring, not scary. Each mile became cooler as the altitude increased and remnants of snow from the previous months remained. Once again, I started to realise that reputations are often absurd.

After a few hours of brutally slow progress, eventually the gradient began to level out, before turning to a fully-fledged descent. This was the top of the mountain. I had made it. I was on top of the world, and wanted to raise my bike into the air like a champion and scream, but it was too heavy and it wasn't a good place to pull a muscle.

I took a break for half an hour to sit and take it in. The view was vast forest, never ending, and you could easily imagine being lost for weeks in there.

Then, whilst descending, I realised why this mountain has a reputation.

Flying. Absolutely flying. Soaring down the back side of one of the biggest hills I'd ever climbed on a bike. Euphoric. My eyes were in a half squint to cope with the wind hitting my face, and my smile at an all time size.

The adult black bear was on the road 20 metres ahead.

I was going too fast to stop, although time did seem to slow.

We looked up and clocked each other at the same time.

The bear made a HUMPHHH sound.

When you make eye contact with a bear at close range, there's a weird human connection that takes place. I swerved nervously onto the other side of the empty road whilst the bear dived into the bushes.

My heart had never beaten as fast.

A short while afterwards, the light was fading when the second bear incident happened.

On a small climb, a young cub was hanging out at the side of the road. In isolation it was quite adorable, like a small puppy. The little cub was just exploring.

But it takes a nano-second, from coming across a bear cub, to literally praying that you haven't accidentally stumbled in between the cub and it's mother. The logic behind 'big animals are more scared of us than we are of them' is generally true, until you pose a threat to the mother by sandwiching yourself in between her and her child. Those are the moments when humans get mauled.

Looking around, panicked, suddenly the brand new record for fast heartbeat that had only just been set, had already been broken.

There wasn't an adult bear within eyesight, so I got off the bike, and slowly walked past the cub. It had a brief look of con-fusion in its eyes, until it jovially bounded off to the side of the road and up the hill.

After a while I made it to the nearest town of Lillooet and camped in the park, strangely on edge from the day that had been. Mount Currie had earned it's reputation.

23

Trouts And Waiting

WOBBLING IN, ON A WHEEL THAT WAS NOW COMPLETELY done in, the closest I came to having a mental breakdown was in Prince George, British Columbia.

All spare spokes had been used up. They kept snapping. The wheel had turned from circular to, well, not very circular at all.

Riding into the city, after an absolute mission in the pouring rain, I got my bearings at a Tim Hortons. Tim's is Canada's most prominent donut / coffee chain. They're located in most of Canada's towns and cities, so they soon became my Canadian home away from home.

Still drenched, it was a pleasant surprise to see that two separate people had replied to a WarmShowers message that was sent out a couple of days before, to say that they'd be willing to provide a place to stay.

I'd ordered a new wheel from Steve the policeman's basement, but it wasn't due to arrive at the post office for another few days, so having the opportunity to sleep indoors was a blessing.

In Tim Horton's, a Londoner who had moved to the city in pursuit of a lucrative career in the forestry industry told me to move on quickly. He was adamant that "Prince George is like the armpit of BC. It's just really, really shit."

But we all know not to judge a book by it's cover, and that reputations are often skewed. And regardless of whether the city was "really, really shit", the plan was to be here only briefly anyway. A couple of days, three at the most, just like most other places. However, little did I know that the wheel would take 17 days to show up.

A woman called Barb was one of the people who'd replied to the WarmShowers message, and she happily said that there was a truck camper in her driveway which was available, and it was only ten minutes away from the centre.

Barb worked at a bank in Prince George. She was married to Les, who also worked in the forestry industry. On the side they ran a quilting company with an enormous industrial quilter in their front room that had laser guides and pedals. My dad would've loved the machine and my mum would've loved the quilts it made.

They were immediately very kind, a real standout host experience. On the first night Barb and Les had setup a huge barbecue in the garden where we ate, drank Hungarian beer, and played fetch with their dog as night fell.

It's crazy how often you miss variety in food when you're on the road all the time. Stove food is not the same, nor is fast food - all that becomes quite boring, and something you eat rather than enjoy. So this barbecue was bliss. There was corn on the cob, steak, everything. I'm drooling as I write this. The keyboard is literally wet.

The truck camper was essentially a big caravan that sat on the bed of Les's pickup truck. They're surprisingly roomy, essentially a mini apartment, with a bed, a kitchen, a table, a bathroom.

As it became obvious that something was causing the wheel delivery to be increasingly delayed, life in Prince George became trying. A recurring theme developed. Every day started with the same routine: going into town, checking with the post office to see whether anything had arrived and being told 'no' and to 'try again tomorrow'. This continued until I eventually got hold of a tracking number.

The package had gotten caught up in customs, and was being held in Vancouver. I kicked myself for ordering something from the US instead of getting it locally. But knowing that the parcel had already been sent out, it seemed reasonable to wait. And wait.

I tried to occupy myself with touristy things, but there wasn't a whole lot going on in Prince George. There's a lot to do when it snows, but in the summer, not so much. In hindsight, maybe there is actually plenty to do, but I'd begun to enter a dark patch so I became blind to any of it.

Les mentioned casually one evening that he loves to fish. Fishing always seemed to me to be something that people do when they're content. So it seemed like a great idea to head out to the lake - to unwind, and to escape the Prince George post office trap.

We arrived at the lake, after a short drive listening to Santana on loud, blaring out of the pickup truck in the sunshine. Les unloaded the boat from the roof of the truck and set it up with everything needed for a couple of hours of fishing, before we pushed it out into the lake and jumped in to the metal frame.

He cast out, far into the green water.

My experience with fishing is limited, however I do remember going through a fishing phase as a ten year old and never catching anything. Possibly that's been engrained subliminally, because I was skeptical of our chances.

A mere two minutes after putting the boat in the water, Les caught a trout. Turns out people are able to actually catch fish in reel life. Les caught fish after fish after fish, with absolute ease.

He handed me the rod. We had to be discreet and quick because apparently there might be strict rangers out in force, and without a fishing license they wouldn't be very happy.

Watching Les a moment before, it seemed like it was literally impossible not to catch a fish today. So the pull of the line wasn't surprising. It must be a fish. This would be the first fish I ever caught. Ray Mears would've been proud. I began to reel it in. It would probably be a trout big enough to feed a family for a month. The tug on the line got a little lighter, but maybe that's just what happens as the enormous fish gets closer to the surface.

Then out it came, attached to the hook.

Weeds from the bottom of the lake.

It was a wonderful afternoon, despite only one of us having success, and it was refreshing to try something new and to connect with someone in a way that wasn't the typical fleeting conversation. There's nothing fleeting about being on a small boat.

Les was quiet and introverted, but had a wiseness when he spoke. We spoke about ambition and contentment. It was a theme that came up a lot.

"As long as you find a few small things that make you happy, and can figure out a way to do them, then that's all anyone can and should ask for," he said.

Fishing over, we returned to Prince George and I continued the post office routine, being based out of the truck camper for a few more nights.

We all know about the invisible line that is hospitality. I was aware that the longer I stayed in the truck camper, the closer I was getting to that line. As a dirty traveller, more than two nights seemed like it was pushing it with a single host, let alone the six that it had been so far. It wasn't fair on the hosts, so I felt a strong urge to move on and kill time elsewhere. So the next day, I thanked them for the food, the bed, the kindness and the fun day out, and packed up, still without a wheel.

The next few days led to an increasingly frustrated and depressed mood. I wasn't giving the city a chance.

In retrospect, it was Prince George that made me realise that when you believe a situation is bad, you often make it fit your beliefs. What a place is actually like becomes irrelevant when you're in this mindset. Sometimes you sabotage your time in a place, because of first impressions and an unwillingness to dive deeper. It's a trap that's easy to fall into, when you move all the time and grow used to only scratching the surface of a place, and it's a trap I had well and truly entered whilst in the city.

There was a church. Churches had become a safe-place on the trip in the times of not knowing what else to do. Not because of praying or anything like that, but for accommodation. You could often sleep in church grounds without trouble. Either nobody would ever know, or someone would come over, ask what's up, say that it was fine to sleep here and sometimes offer dinner or a place to stay indoors in the church.

Making the decision to sleep in a church was a moral dilemma I was not oblivious to, though. Is it okay to sleep in a church without believing in God? Just using it as a campsite? Maybe it's okay if you only do it occasionally? Maybe it's not okay at all? Relying on church gardens seemed, and still seems, morally questionable.

The doorway of the church was under a shelter. There was a fence ten metres away, with a used car garage on the other side. The concrete floor, inches away from the church's blue front door, would be my bedroom for several of the following nights.

Every day I got up, packed the sleeping gear in to the panniers, and pushed the bike back into the centre for a hopeful change in the postal status. It didn't change, the wheel was still stuck in transit, so I left to try and explore the city some more.

At one point I went back to the church doorway, feeling intensely introverted, and lay on the floor. I read 'Argo' in a single sitting and people walking on the sidewalk near the church would look over and mutter to each other. I imagined them talking about the homeless guy sat in front of the church, assuming that the book he was reading was the bible. Maybe reading the bible instead of Argo would've made sleeping in the church doorway more morally acceptable.

Unsurprisingly, those nights on the concrete in front of the church lead to an intense fatigue.

But all looked up, at bloody last, when the tracking status of the wheel changed. The package was out of customs and was on its way. It was on it's way!

Two days later, it had "been delivered."

There had been a few great people in the city. Barb and Les were both lovely and had shown amazing hospitality, and I'll always be extremely grateful for that. And if you lived there, and took time to explore, dive under the surface, and get to know people, you may be able to make it your own and love it. Maybe Jenn from the coffee shop would become single. All those things would make a huge difference, and in time this place might become home. My dark experiences here had been formed by mindset and nothing else. Here, like everywhere else, people showed extreme generosity to strangers. Having a bad time was my own fault, because I'd ignored that.

But towards the end of the unexpected 17 day stint, my view had been tainted by frustration and the warped feeling that, whilst in the church doorway, I was truly alone. So I genuinely couldn't wait to move on.

On the final day, when I went in to the post office and they said there was a wheel-sized box waiting in the back room, it was one of the most uplifting days I'd had for a long time.

I fitted it, and began riding away with a smile, at last. And about two miles out of the city, the bike's derailleur hanger fucking snapped.

24

Protein And
Grizzly's

PRINCE RUPERT IS A PORT CITY ON THE COAST OF BRITISH Columbia. It's obviously experienced hard economic times and a lot of the shops and buildings are boarded over and derelict. The ferry terminal, just outside of town, was as functional as ever though.

My plan was to board the Alaska Marine Highway - a ferry system that works it's way up this section of coast - and step off in a couple of weeks near Anchorage, Alaska - the state that has, by far, the biggest reputation for being wild, out there, and remote.

The problem was, heading to The Last Frontier meant crossing back in to the US.

The border guard was used to giving people a grilling. It was quite nerve-wracking after all the shenanigans that had taken place in New Mexico a few months ago. He gave me a form to fill out. The ones with the tick boxes that asked you to declare that you weren't a terrorist, weren't carrying a nuclear weapon, or you weren't bringing in exotic animals.

"You just ticked this box," he said in a threatening voice and pointing at the sheet, "so you're saying you don't have any food with you?"

"Oh, sorry. No, yeah, um, I mean yes, I have a little bit."

"Well then how can I believe these other boxes? You have food with you, so you just admitted to a US official that you lied."

He was another Jeremy Jobsworth.

"Oh, sorry. Could I get a new form?"

He looked and contemplated my appearance for a while, realising after an oddly long time that Al-Qaeda or ISIS operatives would probably use a different approach than disguising themselves as long-distance cycling travellers and heading to Alaska.

He handed over a new form.

"Just make sure you read it properly this time!"

The ferry was simply a spectacular experience. Like real Disney movie stuff. The journey to Anchorage, via the cheapest ticket, meant passage would take two weeks, stopping at Wrangell, Petersburg, and Juneau along the way. Sometimes the stop would be for just a day, other times nearly a week. This was a relatively relaxing time. So long as you made the next connection on time, there was little else to worry about.

On the boat, between the towns, was where the magic really happened. I'm not exaggerating when I describe this journey as being like something out of a Disney movie. It was like a fantasy world. The captain would make an announcement, over the ship's PA.

"Ladies and gentleman, coming up on our starboard side is a pod of Orcas. I repeat, pod of Orcas on the starboard side."

Everyone would rush outside to the deck and rest against the railings, cameras in hand. And there they were. A team of killer whales just next to the boat. Their blowholes threw spray into the chilly air, causing vocal oohs and ahhs amongst all onlookers.

The air was bitter, as we made our way North, and the landscape became filled with mountains to the side of the ship. Endless snow-capped peaks stretched as far as the eye could see. It was becoming really wild, already living up to the reputation it had as 'the wild state'. Stepping off the boat seemed like it would mean stepping into a new world. One without a McDonalds or a gas station every few miles.

Creativity was high on that boat. A writing friend recommends taking public transport as a way to get into the zone, and here I understood what she meant. There are no distractions on the water, and you are constrained so have little else to do but be creative. This is a lesson I'll try to take forward - if work seems like a struggle, if possible, cut yourself off for a bit.

Sat out on the deck, however, creative streaks were often interrupted, albeit in an unusual way. A humpback whale would dive into the air, clearing the surface of the water completely. It became airborne and wowed. Entranced, more oohs and aahs were exhaled from passengers.

At last, we reached the final destination of Wrangell near Anchorage, at the crack of dawn, two weeks after stepping aboard. Admittedly, sleeping on the carpet in the lounge of the ferry, combined with stealth camping in each port stop, meant that I was setting off exhausted again. But what's new?

I stepped off, onto land, and had a moment of reflection. The journey felt more real in Alaska, more worthwhile somehow, more of an adventure. It's hard to explain why, but I was part overwhelmed, part more happy than ever, part sad too that this was a solo endeavor because it would've been great to share.

The bike worked again, the new wheel was standing strong and became forgettable - which is exactly what you want in bike hardware.

With each day that went by after leaving Anchorage, the landscape really did become more exposed and exciting. Towns became further apart, and for the first time, there were long stretches of road, with nothing on them other than wild surroundings. This, in itself, made a difference to the whole adventurous feeling, because you had to plan, and you couldn't rely on just popping into a shop up the road. Here, there were 110 mile stretches of nothingness.

I was taking the George Parks Highway route. It's an immense, picturesque road that joins Anchorage to Fairbanks over the course of 360 miles through Denali National Park. It can be a scary place for a solo traveller living in a tent, and the reason for this is Grizzly Bears.

"There's more Grizzly's in Alaska than there are people," would be an often repeated claim.

That's also the big draw, of course. It's not all fear and death and mauling when bears are involved. They are beautiful, incredible creatures. And Denali is renowned for them. Thousands of tourists flock here in the summer to see them from the inside of a bus tour, before heading back to an RV or a hotel.

The stats show that they are rarely dangerous to humans. The chances are akin to a lottery jackpot or being hit by lightning. It's perhaps ridiculous, then, how they still managed to drum up a lot of intimidation and thoughts of getting chewed to death. Constantly camping in prime bear territory puts you into a sense of heightened alertness. That means, night after night, you're on edge. It's always at the back of your mind. So high quality sleep is rarely achieved. And yet again, the cycle of no sleep goes on!

The remote stretches of Alaskan highway were occasionally broken up with the smallest of villages. Rarely very populated, they mostly just contained a tiny gas station and, every so often, a post office. This provided an opportunity, and I did something which I had never felt the need to do before.

It was a moment of desperation, a desire to escape being 'outside' for a few hours, a craving to be surrounded by real walls, a want to forget all animal thoughts and get some rest.

The post office was open! It was 11pm, still light outside, and the post office was open!

Rural post offices in Alaska are always open. Residents have their own keys to a box, and can come and go as they please to collect their post. It's only during regular working hours that the building is manned by staff, so utilising the familiar 'arrive late, leave early' approach, Alaska's post offices were essentially a no-budget luxury hotel.

For two nights, I rolled out a thin foam mat in the corner of a new post office each night, dived into my sleeping bag, drew the hood tight, and hoped there wouldn't be any nocturnal locals who came to collect their letters at silly o'clock. Because the situation might appear a bit weird.

With a slight post office refresh, I continued cycling towards Fairbanks, as Denali, the highest peak in North America, was shrouded in cloud.

Decent nutrition had been lacking for, um, a couple of months. My diet was quite phase-orientated, influenced mostly by convenience, so I usually fell into one of two ways of getting by. One was cold food during the day - cereal bars etc - and then fast food in the evenings. This was fairly cheap and easy, and provided a place to sit inside after a day of riding. The other way was cooking out of the tent. It was hard to drum up the motivation to do this each and every night, but when I did, the meal was usually pasta with mixed in tuna.

Because of the Parks Highway, and the distances in between places, cooking was the most effective way to have an evening meal.

Eggs. The shop only stocked a 24 pack.

As a solo cyclist, is buying 24 easy-to-crack eggs sensible? Probably not.

The till beeped and I walked out, now carrying two dozen eggs.

It made more sense to boil them before cycling away. Far more sensible. That way they wouldn't crack.

My God, the next few days were awful.

I lived purely on bagels, mayonnaise, and chopped up boiled eggs as a filling.

It started off being nice, something new, variety.

It ended up, in those stretches where there was nothing, being absolutely sickening. Foolishly riding into nothingness, carrying no other options except fucking boiled eggs.

I've not eaten a boiled egg since.

25

Finding Magic,
Death And
Happiness

THE MOSQUITOS WERE UNBEARABLE. THE WORST EVER. A big swarm of buzz and self-chosen torture. A constant, itchy white noise. 'Should've taken a net but didn't'.

And that word, HUMAN. The same word over and over again. Saying it enough would drive anyone mad.

Underprepared would be the right word for this situation. That word came up a lot.

The bicycle was locked up behind a Best Western in Fairbanks, and I had decided to switch gears for a few days and see if my legs remembered how to walk instead of pedal.

The Stampede Trail is located just outside Denali National Park, and is 110 miles away from Fairbanks. The trail is notorious, as the location where 'the magic bus' sits. The bus which Christopher McCandless used as a base to live off the land, and the place where it's believed he starved to death. His story had become an internationally well-known one, ever since it was documented in Jon Krakauer's book, and later Sean Penn's film, 'Into The Wild'.

There's a lot that goes through your head when you've been on a solo trip for months. At times it's hard to keep it together. You feel ultimate highs, but you can't escape crushing lows too. Even if you're the most stable person in the world, it's absolutely a bi-polar way of life.

You question the motives of it all. You wonder why you aren't sharing this experience. Wondering if there's something wrong with you for being drawn to this, when in many peoples view it's not normal.

There had been lows recently, brought on, I suspect, by a lack of sleep (surprise, surprise). Once, I threw the bike to the ground, and screamed out 'FUUUUCCCCKKKKKKK', like an irritating melodramatic teenager would do. It wasn't a proud moment.

Mixing it up seemed like a crucial ingredient to make the travelling experience as worthwhile as it could be. Cycling was getting dull in my mind. Doing something different would hopefully provide a refresh, and possibly eradicate those doubtful questions.

So two days earlier, in a typical cheeky Brit way, I stopped pedalling at the most suitable building in Fairbanks, exaggerated an over-the-top accent to 'attempt a Colin Frissell', and asked a team of two receptionists for a favour. The concierge staff of a Best Western agreed to flex the rules because their boss was away, and allowed me to lock up the bike behind the building and shove some gear in their safe. I'm pretty sure they were naturally kind, and that Colin's accent made no difference whatsoever.

The story of Christopher McCandless is a divisive one, but it's touching in many ways. He felt a desire to forgo and reject typical lifestyle security, to be drawn to a life of adventure, experiences, and sustainability. He had a desire for simplicity, for solitude. That's something that is often forgotten in a time when it's so easy to be absorbed by the system and to be busy on our phones and laptops.

There was another side to the story, though. Perhaps a more controversial one, but which was understandable and made a lot of sense. Ever since being in Alaska, I'd been reminded a lot of the distaste the locals have for McCandless. Or more specifically, what he represents.

Many Alaskan's think of a disillusioned dreamer, naive to the realities of surviving in a harsh environment. Foolish. They hate that people come from around the globe and get themselves in trouble - some have been killed - after being spurred on, more often than not, by a Hollywood movie.

For sanity, all of that seemed unimportant. In my mind, it was an interesting story and it happened close by, but mostly, it was something different than damn pedalling.

Arriving at the supermarket in Fairbanks just before it closed, I picked up a pack of granola bars, and began hitchhiking to the start of The Stampede Trail. On my back was a single rucksack, which contained a camera, a small tent, a 5mm foam mat, a water bottle, and the GPS from the bike. It wasn't a large collection of gear, and I chose not to take a sleeping bag, because it was intended to be a light and fast mission. Perhaps this approach was a little too minimal, in hindsight. Ruddy hindsight.

To get to the start of the trail took three separate rides.

The first was with a friendly couple on their way home from a party in Fairbanks who were fun and energetic, pumping the music on the ride but only going a few miles. Another was with a forestry-worker who had just clocked off and was driving to his cabin. He was unusually laid back. The reason why became clear when he insisted on giving me a joint for the trail to "make it truly magical."

The final ride was with an off-duty army officer from the local base. He was driving a black truck with tinted windows. He had dark sunglasses on. It was chilly inside the truck with the air conditioning blasting.

Hitchhiking is this bizarre act, with a reputation for being sketchy and dangerous, when in reality the statistics show the opposite. But people would have you believe that most people who hitchhike, or pick up hitchhikers, are serial killers. That's ridiculous.

But this ride immediately felt tense.

His name was Mike, and when I got in and sat on the leather passenger seat, he immediately locked the doors. Slightly creepy move. He told me that he was on the way to Anchorage for a blow out, and had been on the base for so long recently that he was going to "go to a strip club, then find a prostitute to finally get laid."

The music was heavy metal which added to the tension. Mike didn't speak much. Like a cobra, he quickly struck out a hand to open the glove box. I honestly thought he was going to pull out a weapon, so clenched my fists in preparation for the worst. The bear spray was unreachable, in the back of the truck, and it's pretty obvious that he would've won the fight. And Alaska seems like a perfect place to dump a body.

It was a tense hour. At the trailhead, he slowed down. The doors were still locked. Maybe this was it. Time to die.

"Oh, has the door been locked this whole time?" he said, with surprise. He opened the locks on the doors.

Nothing sketchy had happened. It was all imagination. Of course it was. The truck sped off into the distance and I can only assume Mike reached Anchorage and found a prostitute for a pleasure session a few hours later.

At around midnight I reached the start of the Stampede Trail. That sounds like a foolish approach, but Alaska in July is the land of the midnight sun. It doesn't get dark at all. The sun dips on the horizon and then starts to rise again. Twenty four hour light.

Travelling so lightly, the animal fear was back with a vengeance. With each step further into the backcountry, I had an increasingly strong wish to be carrying a shotgun.

The canister of bear spray attached to my rucksack strap was so small and would not fill anyone with confidence were a bear attempting to chew on them in the night. Spraying a bear with this pepper-flavoured deodorant would be the equivalent throwing a blunt dart at an oncoming hungry lion, surely. Ineffective.

If a bear attempts an attack, the spray is intended to be fired at them, breaking into a big cloud that they run into. It dazes them and is designed to give you time to escape. But spend enough time in Alaska, and there're plenty of stories about people misunderstanding the spray.

Once, a Japanese couple had gone camping in the backcountry and thought that spraying their tent with the spray would act as a repellant, only to find bear cubs licking the flysheet at four in the morning, audibly enjoying the peppery taste.

Another incident was when someone thought the spray canister was similar to mosquito repellant, only to spray himself in the face and fall to the floor, viciously squirming in the dirt.

Accompanying the strategies of camping a long way away from your food and carrying spray, there are some more approaches to animal safety that have been picked up over time. One was to carry the aforementioned shotgun, but you can't get one as a tourist. The other was to make a regular noise, using a bear bell. Or by shouting out a keyword.

Every minute or so you shout this word at a loud volume. The theory, as always, is that big animals are generally more scared of humans than we are of them, so by shouting, you warn them and they avoid you.

When I read online that someone's keyword was 'HUMAN', this word became engrained in my mind. So I shouted HUMAN. Over, and over, and over again.

Walking the trail was an easy task. Navigationally, it had been ATV'd enough that the route was impossible to get wrong. The only difficult part was the mosquitos. They swarmed to provide a sense of claustrophobia and irritation. I hadn't been expecting them as the roads were generally free of such beasts. But away from the road, in the backcountry, and combined with the repetition of 'HUMAN', the mozzy's added to a unique cocktail that could drive anyone completely around the bend.

The major point on the trail is the main river crossing, of the Teklanika River, or 'The Tek'. This river was a significant moment of no return for Christopher McCandless. He crossed it when it was low, in late April 1992. When he tried to walk out three months later, in July, it was too high, so he returned to the bus and died. That happened on the other side of the river to where I was stood before making the crossing, maybe 40 metres away.

The river, like many a mountain, has a fierce reputation. I half-wanted it to seem scary and intimidating. Sometimes I think we actually want obstacles like that to present themselves, so it makes decisions of retreat easier. But the water seemed okay.

Find a thick stick. Put it in front of you. Feet wide. Facing upstream. Become a human tripod, and shuffle across the river. Get ready to ditch your rucksack and swim if needed. Downstream from the crossing is dangerous, so you must get out fast.

I'd read the river reports and the hype that this stretch of water has in July. Yet the shuffle seemed to be working.

It was halfway across when The Tek demonstrated it's power. The strength of the torrent was intense. Twice, my right foot was pushed violently downstream, causing hairy imbalanced moments as my chest dropped to water level. Staying upright all came down to that thick stick. Halfway across, the river offered a glimpse into why it has the reputation that it has.

But half way? When you get half way, you don't stop. I precariously continued stepping diagonally right and backwards, testing each foot placement, and a minute later, when it was done, took a breath and realised that there was a fair amount of blind luck involved in staying upright.

On the banks, I reached into my pocket. I'm not a smoker, but wondered if lighting the joint would be a good idea here, and whether it would help when it came to ignoring the mosquitos. A little giddy, like a teenager smoking for the first time, I reached to get it out and channel my inner Snoop Dogg. The paper was dripping wet and bent in half from the river crossing. The joint was useless.

It's eerie to be in a place where you know something significant has happened. This river was the cause of McCandless' death. My mind formed a picture of what the circumstances may have been like on that day in 1992 when he failed to walk back to civilisation and was shut down by the crossing. The river would've been running high. He would've been starving, ill, tired, and weak. Those are things that would make any person looking at this crossing feel an overwhelming sense of terror and isolation. Anyone would turn around. Frail, it would've looked like, and possibly been, a deathtrap.

The next few hours on the trail were mainly spent in tree lined rocky corridors and walking up dry river beds. In those moments, it was a type of walk that wouldn't be at the top of anyones list for quality. However, sometimes those trees and river beds stopped and the beauty of the area presented itself. Getting closer to 'the magic bus', it began to be more magical. Open tundra, with colourful plant life, and birds flying high, with the magnificent and now visible Denali National Park range providing a jaw-dropping backdrop.

There it was.

The trail opened, as I walked in to the natural courtyard, with the number 142 bus nestled in the back.

The Magic Bus is a place which has come to represent something. To many it represents youthful adventure, questioning the status quo. And tragedy too.

As far as experiences go, it was quite eerie, more so than the banks of the river. I was happy to be there, at the destination, a mini-goal accomplished, something different to cycling.

But that seemed irrelevant when thinking about the backstory and what had happened here. Christopher had died right there, on the bed that's been built at the back of the bus.

It's been years now, since he died and the story has become well-known. In that time, the trail has seen lots of traffic. It shows - the bus has been vandalised, bullet holes in the exterior, windows put through, and many parts gone. But there's also signs of hospitality. There's emergency food and blankets. Inside there's a visitor book with a note from Christopher's sister, Carine. The pages brim with tales from those who have come here. People from Japan to Nebraska, England to Egypt.

The Magic Bus is a place that people are drawn to when they want to explore a new ideology of simplicity, or when they just want to get away from it all.

Getting to the bus had been sore and stressful, it had taken 15 hours of constant movement and I was knackered. But exploring the pages of the book, and sat in the cabin that had featured death, I realised how at any other time of year, or when ill, this would be an entirely different proposition.

Written down by hand were reports of people using this as a base to spend entire winters. Months here, every day in darkness. In winter this was the land of no sun. Fire would provide the heat, the light and an escape from the snow. I can't imagine a more lonely place than the bus in winter, or when sick.

It was too creepy to sleep inside the bus, so I camped outside, on edge most of the night and sporadically shouting that damn word HUMAN. The word became so irritating that the only option left was to choose something else. Something deep and gritty. Raw. Terrifying.

For some reason the only other thing I could come up with was the lyrics to 'Chocolate Rain' by Tay Zonday. If you search online for that song you'll understand what a ridiculous choice it is.

Try to picture the scene. A couple of plants rustle outside, far away from anything, or anybody else. A scared British voice, thinking the rustles are actually enormous hungry bears, sings out into the nothingness, "Chocolate rain, some stay dry while others feel the pain." You can probably imagine how scared any nearby grizzly bears must've been. Not at all, probably.

Finally my body took over and I couldn't stay awake any longer. A mind-cloud of inevitable sleep encroached. If a hungry bear came, at least I'd be too tired to notice.

The following morning, thankfully still living, I packed up the tent and heard whistling, which was surprising. Eric stumbled into the natural courtyard as I packed the tent away. He'd come from Minnesota and was walking the trail, to the bus and back, in a single day. That's totally nuts, but he was training for a triathlon in a few weeks.

He was a commercial pilot and had made use of his free flights to fly into Fairbanks, walk The Stampede Trail and then head home straight afterwards. This was his second attempt. The first, with his cousin the previous year, had been thwarted by a Tek that was too high to be safe.

Eric talked about what drew him to make a second attempt.

"You know, Alaska's kind of this wild frontier," he said, as he sat on the chair outside the Bus that McCandless had sat in in one of his last self-portrait photographs. "The story just intrigued me after reading the book and seeing the movie, and I can kinda relate to wanting to go out into nature, and hiking out to the middle of nowhere... And the chance of coming out here myself was something I've wanted to do for the last three years. I think the most fascinating part of the story is, he kind of realised that he was doing all this stuff on his own, but at the end he realised that he needed to share experiences with other people. It was really sad and unfortunate that he didn't realise that until it was too late."

Sitting for an hour, we drank sour chlorine-cleaned river water from the Teklanika crossing, until all that was left to do was to plaster up the ever-growing blisters, and limp out of there. We hoped the Tek hadn't suddenly risen, and that all the mosquitos had been murdered in the night. Thankfully the river was fine. The little terrors remained though. One silver lining, though, was that there's a lot less bear-stress when two of you are involved.

Eric had a hire car waiting for him at the start of the trail, so he kindly offered a ride back to Fairbanks, which was a touch of luck because neither of us were in a good way at all. We were truly hobbling, knackered, entirely done in. Eric had just covered the distance of an ultra-marathon over a days walking. Beast. So it worked out well for both of us - he appreciated another body on the drive to Fairbanks to stop him falling asleep at the wheel, and I was so thankful not to hitchhike again with a potential serial killer.

When we got to Fairbanks, it was late. The next three days straight were spent based in a motel, limping, blistered, itching mosquito bites and barely able to move. Every muscle that walking had used was excruciating, and I was over the moon to never shout any keywords again.

It had been a memorable trip, scary and frustrating at times, but it was easy to see that it had been worthwhile. The reason why can be whittled down to just one thing, just one lesson. The one that McCandless learned, and the one that Eric talked about.

Regardless of what stance you take on McCandless and his story, in his last moments one of his final written notes read, "Happiness only real when shared" and there's something important in that for everyone.

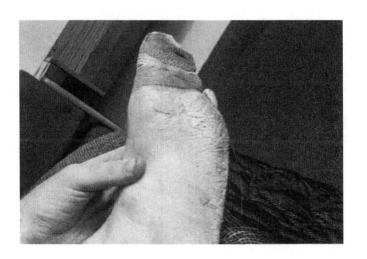

26

North Korea
And Santa

IT HAD BEEN APPARENT FOR THREE HOURS, BUT THE VOMIT exploding from my mouth into the bush reaffirmed that something was wrong. On Santa Claus Lane, in North Pole, a suburb of Fairbanks, and having recently ridden past a reindeer farm, this was, essentially, puking in Santa's garden.

Ill and worn out ever since getting back from The Stampede Trail, I hadn't moved from the motel room for a few days, other than a trip to the laundry and a regular walk 100 metres to a shop that sold chicken burgers and loaves of bread.

Laying on the bed, with an intense headache and joints that ached, I moved only when something horrible that begins with

'D' and kind of rhymes with 'North Korea' kicked in. Figured it out? Yep, gross. Maybe it was something in the river water.

Fairbanks had been the final corner of the journey. Heading North was over. It was now the final stretch East, all the way across Canada and back to the US coast.

The plan was simply to head to Whitehorse, Yukon. That marked the start of riding across Canada. During those bed-ridden days, I delved into Google Maps and was reminded that, by far, the final leg was the longest one and probably the toughest one. That was a little bit intimidating, because the scale of the trip had already seemed quite vast, yet there was an enormous distance still to cover. For that reason, combined with a cracking headache, it took a while to pluck up the motivation and willpower to begin.

On leaving the motel, after just a few minutes I hit a wall and knew it would be a struggle for a few days before getting back into it. Puking in Santa's garden only confirmed that.

CRACK.

"Oh sod off, not now," I muttered as the chain snapped. It was always fairly easy to know when it was coming, because the drivetrain would skip frequently, which was a giveaway sign.

This wasn't too unusual, so I rested the bike against a lamppost and rummaged around to dig out the chain splitter. This time around, it went like this: Kneel down to begin to short fix the chain, quickly get up and run to the bushes to vomit, return to try again, repeat a couple of times until the chain was together again and the bushes looked gross.

In Alaska, navigation on the roads is simple. The options are limited. To get to Whitehorse, for now I just followed Highway 2 - the road which traced the Tanana River upstream. Going upstream means inevitable long hill climbs, but it was never steep, and so was simple to fall into a relaxed state.

Getting into a state of flow on a bike is so awesome. Everything becomes easy, and the clarity that pours into your mind is incredible. That must be why some people are so dedicated to meditation, because they consistently reach this state of mind. There is a drawback though, and that can be that you become so engrossed in your own world that you miss stuff. I'm glad that

I was snapped out of the flow and didn't just keep riding, head down and into the distance. Because there it was. Pulling over into a viewing spot overlooking the river, on the horizon was a perfect view.

The sky was clear and Denali was on display. Formidable snowy ridges were on show, home to epic mountaineering adventures over the years. The other mountains in the range surrounded it, as Denali itself sat in the middle, the king amongst everything else, and glowing in orange light. It could not have been more majestic. And I'm proud to say that Denali didn't make me vomit.

It's very easy to get demoralised by sickness when you're alone. The internal question of "what are you even doing this for, anyway?" again becomes prevalent. A question to which it was always hard to give a good answer.

Thankfully, with improved health, it's easier to remember perspective, which reminds you that suffering is healthy in many ways, and the dark patches add to the overall experience. Give it time and the shit bits become valuable.

On the road headed East, between the small town of Tok Junction and the tiny one of Northway Junction, two cyclists were pedalling on the same stretch of road, and in the same direction, which had become unheard of recently. The simple act of a long conversation with people who are drawn to something similar is a huge lift, and can make you feel far less weird.

Michael and Busy were cruising, heading fast and regularly putting in big days. They were former university pals from Colorado and North Carolina, and were taking a month over their summer break to ride a loop from Anchorage, to Fairbanks, to Whitehorse, and to Juneau.

Like any hobby or sport or clique, bicycle travel has it's fair share of snobs. People who are quick to tell you that "there's a far better route" or "you should get XYZ gear." I was always a little anxious whenever speaking to a hardcore bicycle traveller, and even after 9 months on the road, still felt quite out of place when speaking to the truly dedicated. It was always a relief when most people were not snobby, and if anything, it seemed that a lot of the other actively travelling cyclists were equally put off by 'the snobby ones' who could mostly be found online.

So as Michael and Busy approached, this thought was gladly eradicated when they laughed about how we were all in cotton t-shirts and regular, loose trousers.

"Wahey, another member of the say-no-to-spandex team!" Busy shouted.

We rode together for a while, and the afternoon was full of healthy banter. They were jokers, riding for fun, and to create memories.

A huge lorry passed by, almost clipping Busy, and he gave the driver the finger. We rode, and it was quite obvious that they were fast. For the first time in a long time, just by keeping up, the riding seemed really physical. That was pretty rare unless "a mountain" climb was involved.

They say buses come in pairs. And lo and behold, another cyclist became visible in the distance. You go for weeks without seeing a soul on the road, and then three riders come along at once.

Wish was from Taiwan. When we met, the look in his eyes was quite recognisable. It was a look of "what have I got myself in to?" He had just started his trip, on day two of his long ride, from Fairbanks to Whitehorse and then down the West coast all the way to San Diego. Those first couple of weeks can be tough. You are in pain, a bit scared, and constantly feeling out-of-your-depth. Luckily it's also during this period that you learn, fast, how to get by.

We split up naturally as evening fell. Busy and Michael had their sights set to a camp far along the road, Wish stopped to set up an early camp, and I kept plodding along until, at the top of a hill, my bloody chain snapped again.

This part of Alaska was covered with dark trees, burnt by the annual forest fires. The tree corpses loomed imposingly at either side of the quiet road.

In the middle of a large climb I stood up to pedal with force, which was a decision that came with instant regret.

"OW! FUCK!"

It was a scream not of frustration, not of another snapped chain, but of raw physical agony. I threw the bike down into the grass, and hopped around like a maniac trying not to put pressure on my right leg. During that single pedal stroke, a searing pain whizzed down my hamstring and behind my kneecap.

I hobbled to a gravel turnout, used for forestry access, ripped the camping mat from the elasticated strings on the pannier rack, and threw it onto the gravelly road, collapsing in a heap of despair.

During 252 days on the road, there had been very few physical injuries. So it was a pretty good ratio really. The only other injury of note happened in Charleston, South Carolina. That was a bruised metatarsal, which my physio Graham quickly diagnosed over email, and fixed remotely by advising that I stand on a golf ball. I wondered whether he was playing a practical joke, but it worked wonders.

On the side of the road, all my pressure was now firmly on my left leg only. The road was quite deserted, and I deeply hoped that someone would drive past soon.

A 4x4 slowed down. It was pulling a rickety metal trailer with an impressive Harley-style motor bike propped up inside. A motorbike often seemed appealing. The driver pulled down his window, seeing the thumb that I was needily waving around on the roadside like a psycho, and asked where I was going. Inside the vehicle was the driver, who sported a grizzly, cold appearance, and two women who seemed much more friendly.

"Throw your bike in the trailer and climb in after it then," he said, explaining that they were heading a few towns East and that there was no room in the cabin. "Make a hand signal in the mirror to let me know when to stop."

What followed can only be described as a very bouncy, DIY roller coaster ride. Rattling around inside the loose trailer, the driver roared along as I clung to the edges. The pressure of his foot upon the accelerator pedal was clearly increasing, and it was difficult to avoid sliding around. The hitchhike didn't last long but definitely provided an unusual adrenaline kick, even more so than the mountain bike trail in Alabama.

The main reason why it was so intense was that, as we approached the border that splits the US and Canada, the road surface completely changed. Solid concrete transitioned to loose, muddy track, and combined with a fast driver, it made for a memorable bounceathon, and one which, for a brief while, made the recent thoughts of knee and leg pain fade.

27

Shitting On
The Chairs

M ARBLE SIZED HAIL STONE RATTLED DOWN FROM THE
sky. Real Noah's Ark stuff. With a hobble, I pushed the
bike to a lay-by, and hid in a standalone concrete toilet block,
waiting for the lightning to stop and for a higher being to finish
throwing icy rocks from the sky above.

With the new injury, plus this, everything was going tits
up. It was even tempting to sit on the cold floor and heat up a
bowl of soup just so I could cry into it. That's what people do
sometimes, isn't it?

Using a left leg to provide all the pressure, I'd jumped out of
the 4x4 roller coaster ride and progressed through the border
into Beaver Creek, a small Canadian settlement that felt a lot like

a saloon town in a Western movie. Quickly setting up camp in a park, I reasoned that maybe, possibly, hopefully, sleeping off the injury would make everything good again, come the morning.

Waking in a haze, yawning, I unzipped the tent. There was a man with a pickaxe raised above his head, about to strike into the tent.

'WOAH! WHAT ARE YOU DOING?'

I'd completely forgotten that the previous night involved setting up camp in a park which had statues of local farming figures. The tent was pitched directly under a statue of a farmer with a pickaxe raised above his head, which provided a unique and terrifying start to the day.

For days, the hail turned to rain which turned back to lightning.

There was a hotel down the road from the park. As the sky poured, I used the bike as a Zimmer Frame, and hobbled towards it. Even if not staying in them, hotels were useful. They have shelter and wifi. The network is usually unlocked, or protected by a password that is 'password'.

Stumbling into an annexed laundry building, I sent off a descriptive email to Graham at The Body Rehab back in the UK to see if he had any advice, and whether there was an easy fix to this injury. As the rain battered down, I sat with a lack of focus in the laundry for hours. It was quite a lonely place to be, but beat being outside.

There is always a point of sitting around aimlessly for too long on the road, when you say to yourself "What are you doing? This is not why you're here! Get up! Move!" But it was hard to know what else to do. Usually in times like this, you pedal on and things work out, but the leg was putting a stop to that.

Up came the thumb again.

Back in Northern California, before stepping on the bus in Eureka, I knew that breaking the cycle in a major way with motorised transport would likely make future decisions of taking an easy way out much easier. These kind of decisions had become, subliminally, much easier.

Reaching Whitehorse would wipe 277 miles from the journey, but I reasoned (and firmly clung to any sense of reasoning) that the city would be a better place to rest and figure this out.

After half an hour, an RV stopped.

Valerie and Joni had been in Alaska for three weeks. They were in their sixties, were lifelong friends, and this trip had been Joni's first time ever away outside of her home state of Florida, so for that reason alone it had been a meaningful experience for them both. They were now on their way home, driving back to Valerie's base in Southern Washington, via Whitehorse.

"Jump in," said Valerie. "We actually drove past once and had to turn around. We couldn't leave someone standing in the rain like that!"

They were both sat in the front of the huge RV, and when opening the door to the main interior, three tiny white puppies started yelping. Cramming the bike through the small gap, we set off, and in return for a ride all the way to Whitehorse, I had been tasked with one thing.

"Just make sure the dogs don't shit on the chairs," Joni laughed.

Deal. These ladies didn't mess around with their words. This was going to be fun.

"Help yourself to anything back there!" Valerie shouted. There was fruit. Sandwiches. Jerky. Coke. And the dogs didn't look like they were going to shit on the chairs anytime soon.

For the next few hours, we had long conversations under the cover of reggae music. Everyone had to shout to communicate over the roar of the rickety engine noise and the yelps of the dogs.

Joni admitted that even though she had enjoyed her first ever travelling experience, she'd had enough now, and was looking forward to going home.

"The constant sunlight has totally screwed with my head. I'm tired and want to go home," she admitted. I found it easy to connect with this. Constant light is a blessing and a curse. Like Joni, I was glad that nights were getting dark from about 10.30pm now.

Valerie explained that she now lived in the RV, and has given up having a home base. She used to be a lecturer but had recently retired, and was enjoying a lifestyle that allowed spending a few weeks in one place and then moving on to somewhere new.

"Do you get tired of it?" I asked, knowing that the road life can be an exhausting one.

"Sure, sometimes," she said. "Like at the moment, my daughter is getting married so I'm going to head back to Florida to settle for a while, and I'm looking forward to that. But I love moving and the simplicity. The stress is there, but it's simple stress. Whenever it gets bad, I think back to the reasons why I'm choosing to live like this."

The direction of this conversation became suddenly sensitive, as though it was bringing up dark memories from deep down. So we moved on and the volume of the Bob Marley CD seemed to increase a lot.

We were passing through spectacular scenery. Soaring to the side of us were steep sided valleys, filled in their centre with dark lakes. In the sun, every cyclist would look at this as a great, memorable place to ride. There'd be moose roaming around and it would be incredible.

In contrast to that, though, we passed a cyclist who was face to the floor, tenaciously tackling a large hill next to the huge Kluane Lake, with his raincoat hood done up tightly around his helmet.

Being in the RV felt like the easy way out, of course it did, and even rare decisions like this made me feel like a massive fraud. 'The adventure is happening outside, not here', the internal monologue would conclude. Surely a decision like hitchhiking in an RV took away from the overall experience of the journey.

In time, I realised that dedicating time - a long period of it - to something, is often what makes it special, and these blips of making the immediate experience easier can actually add massive amounts of value to the overall one. It makes me laugh now that, at the time, these decisions could cause angst. Such moments, in retrospect, become highlights, not cop-outs. But still, at the time, as we passed the cyclist I had a twinge of guilt.

When we pulled in to Whitehorse, Valerie pulled over at a strip mall as night began to fall. Yet another moment of great generosity had just taken place. And the chairs were still dog shit free.

I thanked Joni and Valerie and hobbled off to find shelter. It was really pouring down, and no potential hosts on WarmShowers had replied. But there was a Home Depot.

The building was closed and there was nobody around, so I pitched the tent under a metal fire escape. Any budget for 'real accommodation' was increasingly tight as the trip went on, and even though camping outside a Home Depot is clearly a terrible decision, I climbed into my makeshift home and tried to sleep. Even more than the laundry room, it was a depressing place to be.

As the rain battered down, a puddle surrounded the tent like a pond, which made things even more cold and uncomfortable.

You may be able to tell that it was becoming easy to fall into self-pity mode, and that night led to a bit of a breakdown. The misery kicked in. The questions of 'why' became prominent again. Everything was becoming tiresome, and apart from odd bits and bobs, the previous couple of weeks had rarely been enjoyable. Motivation for each day was getting harder to come by. Knackered most of the time, living in a zombie-state, I wanted to sack it all off.

Ready for hindsight again? Those struggles, and 'the suffering' is a massive part of the appeal. But you don't think like that when you're living it, in the trenches of your own mind, and at Home Depot I was moments away from quitting.

In the morning, crawling out on to the concrete, I stuffed everything miserably into the pannier bags. At a local McDonalds, an email from Graham was waiting. He thought the injury could be related to overuse, and advised ice, rest, stretching of the quads, and inflammatories for a few days as an initial step. But fuck, that meant waiting around, and I didn't want to go through another night like the Home Depot one ever again.

Karma or fate or coincidence or something has a way of arriving at just the right time. Or maybe you only notice it when things work out. Either way, that morning an email pinged in and I was paid for a magazine job from two months earlier. It wasn't much but was enough to hide from the bloody rain and get a shoddy motel bed for a few nights. And shoddy, when you live on a bicycle, is not shoddy at all, it's 5 star. You know what they say. Money can't buy happiness, but it can buy a motel room which is better than concrete in the rain.

On walking into the foyer, the receptionist said "you look really tired." That phrase was starting to become a bit of a tagline. You have to be willing to take the low points if you're going to take the high ones.

28

Reality And
Covering It Up

A FEW WEEKS LATER, NOW HAVING MADE IT TO BRITISH Columbia, all was well in the leg department. That blip was over. Graham's advice had saved the day, and injuries were non-existent again. But the tiredness didn't stop, and ever since Home Depot night, I struggled to climb out of the hole that was depression and exhaustion.

Throughout July, and into August, was the toughest period of time on the road. Yet somehow, it was weirdly frightening to be entirely truthful about the lows. So I'd been putting up a front, attempting to present the trip in a positive manner through blog posts.

In Fort St John - a place that, in my mind, seems much more worthy of being called "the armpit of British Columbia" than anywhere else, I snapped.

The words I'd been writing online hadn't always been true, and for anyone who was genuinely interested in this kind of journey, they deserved an honest portrayal of the mental side to this way of life. They should know that it's not glamorous, and doesn't involve unicorns and candy-floss mountains. Plus, the act of venting can be healthy. So to push the weight off my chest, I posted a new blog. A problem shared is a problem halved and all that.

Posted to VagueDirection.com on August 11th, 2013:

"To post or not to post? For the last month or so, the content that has been published on this blog has been covering up the reality to avoid negativity. It's easier to be positive if you just focus on what's been happening in front of your eyes instead of behind them. And who wants to read a negative post, really? There's enough negativity in the world without yet another blog joining the bandwagon. But covering up the truth in fake positivity is disengaging and it's see-through. And maybe writing this stuff down will be therapeutic.

There's been emails from people saying things like "Savour every moment", and "You're living my dream!" And I just think about how ghetto it is, or the hour every night spent finding a place to sleep. Waking up in lay-by's and car parks day after day, week after week, is not something to savour.

It isn't glamorous, and there are times when I sit on the grass in the morning, looking at the bike with resentment. Why did I sign up for this?

In retrospect I'll look back on this as 'living the dream', for sure. There are times now that I look back on with such fondness. The first 4 months – one of the best periods of my life. No doubt. A bike ride across a continent and a trip that has brought me together with some amazing people and incredible moments. Pinch-me, how-on-earth-did-this-happen moments.

But it can be so draining, demoralising and depressing, even when you're in the most amazing areas. And there's times when I think about those emails and think, it should be them doing this, not me. I'm a fraud and they're not. They'd wake up stoked about pedalling all day, whereas I go through phases of waking up with dread. What's the point in yet more days in the saddle? The tough parts are pedalling every day to get anywhere, and having to find a new place to sleep, dry out, wash and escape the rain, every single day. That quickly adds up.

I always looked at 'adventurers' with a hint of annoyance. They'd use terms like 'quest' and publish 'memoirs' about their time away. It would often hum of pretension and schmuck, and in more-than-a-few cases I got the feeling that their adventures were more about public speaking gigs than the actual experience. Even now, when somebody refers to themselves as an adventurer it makes me shudder. I'd read the blogs, and just didn't buy it. Wasn't this just hyperbole designed to appeal to a reality TV audience who didn't know any better?

They'd talk about how mentally tough it had been, and I'd think, hang on a minute, you're rowing across an ocean in a boat with a Sat Phone and pinpoint navigation, all you do is row, it can't be that hard. Get-bloody-on-with-it or stop complaining and quit if you don't want to be there.

The real adventurers were those who operated under the radar – they'd sail to uncharted lands at a time before GPS, flares and helicopter rescue, or escape from a prisoner of war camp and walk for a year through the jungle, battling anacondas and avoiding the arrows of tribesmen. The explorers who fought pirates with swords. They were heroes, rather than self-branded, media-savvy "adventurers." And they got on with it, rather than purposefully trying to grow an audience by telling everyone how epic it was. I thought that in a modern and connected world, adventure was nearly impossible to find.

And then I set off on this trip and my opinion didn't change. If anything it was reinforced initially. It wasn't hard. It was sore but never unbearable. You're connected almost everywhere. But then after a while, slowly my opinion did start to change.

It's not the physical side that makes a hardcore adventure. You don't have to walk through the jungle for 18 months or fight pirates. It's 100% mental, and unique to each person. It's the toll of time, not the toll on your body. Overcoming the demons that grow in your head and scream at you to stop and call you a freak. It's arduous, and committing to the time is an intimidating thing, even after nine months.

My subconscious constantly asks "what's the point of what you're doing?" It's ignoring that question, or trying to answer it, that's challenging. It's keeping going.

It's this weird way of life where nothing is moderate. It's great or it's shit. Rarely it's in between. Honestly, there's no place I'd rather be most of the time. I feel a sick and twisted attraction to the mental game. But at the same time, sometimes it's the polar opposite of enjoyable. That's strange and full of hypocrisies, I know, but it seems to be the curse of movement, the road, and living a stripped down life that at the moment is literally strapped to a set of wheels. There are no sides – I love it and hate it at the same time.

This project has totally changed how I view adventure – it is real. And if it is mental, then this is most certainly a really wild adventure. But it's still not a quest, okay?"

It was really scary to hit publish. Scary because parts of it were hypocritical. I had a blog so was plenty "media-savvy", and you are reading this in a book, after all! But scary, also, because I wondered if people would read it and think of someone who was complaining about something that they'd give anything to be able to do.

I hit the button, packed up my computer, and cycled off to find another stealth camp.

I needn't have worried. Turns out writing honestly can a) be stress relief in itself, and b) can make you realise that people actually recognise journeys can get hard sometimes, and they appreciate the openness.

There were quite a few comments on this blog post, which did absolute wonders to pick up my spirit which was at an all time low. One from a reader called Eiljah meant a lot:

"...I was on the road for 5 years on and off, and I can resonate with your sentiments," he wrote. "I feel like my experience at first WAS glamorous, but as days turned to months, dread was the theme. I felt like the eyes that would gaze at me only saw the dirt that stuck to my gear and clothes, and my conversations started to become a depressing story of meaningless wanderlust. All in all, I would say that if I were to take on some more touring in the future, it would have to be with a group, and not too extended; maybe across the country at best. My heart goes out to you, and I hope that meaningful thoughts, and compassionate actions arise in your journey. Extended isolation is trying, to say the least."

It's amazing how brief comments can be quite moving, or uplifting. I realised, for the first time, that there were people who understood, who knew about the good and the bad. And knowing that there were people on this journey vicariously helped eradicate thoughts of selfishness and weirdness for a while.

In spirit, other people were along on this journey too, and it was quite moving to realise that.

29

A Burt Reynolds
Disaster

A VENT IS ONE WAY TO GET BETTER. THAT'S ALL IT TOOK TO perk up, and for parts of the journey not to be mental torture anymore. Actually, it went further than that. I felt invincible, which again demonstrates the fluctuating, bi-polar life that is the road.

Prairie life was starting to begin. I'd already experienced the infamous flat farmland for a while, but just outside of the city of Edmonton is where it truly began for a sustained stretch of about 1,000 kilometers.

Mentally, the reputation of The Prairies was fierce, according to a few other cyclists. Some would tell horror stories about beginning to cycle across Canada, but giving up as they got so bored of the monotony that they rode to the nearest bus stop and went home, preferring this to eventually 'blowing their brains out due to boredom.' The nickname, "The Tedious Prairies" had been mentioned twice.

So all things considered, ignoring Edmonton, as the last pit-stop for a while, seemed like a mistake. After all, the North West corner of North America had kicked the proverbial shit out of me, and I wasn't going to waste this opportunity.

What a blast it was.

Amie and Alberto replied to a WarmShowers message with a big smiley invitation to crash at their house. Arriving at their new home, which they'd literally moved into that morning, they were preparing a mind-blowing dinner. Scattered amongst the empty rooms, were moving boxes marked with Sharpies. They'd graciously offered the use of their basement as an apartment for a couple of days, and were very keen, but thankfully not intense, cyclists.

I dumped the bike in the garage, and Alberto lent a hand carrying gear to the basement. Inside was a bathroom and a mattress. Amie handed over a key to the house, for when the couple were at work. Even though moments of insane hospitality weren't rare any more, total trust amongst strangers continued to blow my mind.

It could not have been a better time to be in the city. As we ate dinner, Amie explained why the city was so busy. The Edmonton Fringe Festival was happening, a cultural festival in the old town which is Canada's equivalent to The Edinburgh Fringe. It draws people from around the country to comedy, street performers, and late nights. The festival provided a setting to have fun. It also provided a setting to make an embarrassing mistake.

Whilst Amie and Alberto were at work the following day, I slowly rode (without panniers, at long last) to the Old Town. Finding a discreet bike rack, I locked up the steed, and with just a rucksack on my back, began to explore.

It had become habit to carry the rucksack around. In it, always, was a camera, audio equipment, a laptop and hard drives with the footage and photos that had been collected along the journey. Known as the 'vital bag', the number one rule was that it should never be separated from my person, because within it was sentimental value that was priceless, and could never be obtained again. I would even sleep with it strapped to my arm.

The streets were amass with liveliness and bustle. There were 20 minute shows where people on stilts did backflips and juggled fire and wowed their audience. Entertainers would ask you to hold ropes. Everybody would clap and give a donation. The atmosphere brimmed with lightheartedness.

Outdoor performances began drawing in for the evening, so I found a place in the corner of a sports bar. Months before, hanging out alone at places like this would have caused a minor panic attack. Not knowing anyone and clearly being alone in public can sometimes be uncomfortable, and can take some getting used to. But as the months had passed, so too had a knowledge that exposing yourself to intimidating situations often leads to a worthwhile experience. That, and a tired irreverence when it came to judgement.

The bar was heaving because of the festival, but the waitresses still went from customer to customer with ease, taking orders and making small talk. I ordered a drink. All the cringeworthy stories have that line, and this is no exception to the rule.

Two Spanish girls came into the bar and sat down on the next two bar stools. They were Sofia and Claudia and they ordered BBQ chicken wings. Both were quite attractive. Someone might even call them drop-your-drink-on-the-floor-attractive. The girls I mean, not the chicken wings. Those might well cause a similar adjective too, but they were yet to be brought out so it was impossible to tell.

Sofia was upbeat, happy. She had mousey brown hair and was very rock and roll, coming to town just for a couple of days from Calgary, where Claudia and herself were on a year-long exchange at the university.

It can be a bit creepy when a lonesome dude is sat in a busy bar. I was quite aware of that, and was becoming increasingly self-conscious so didn't plan on sticking around long. Sofia and Claudia sat down on the opposite side of the bench. When the wings arrived, there was more on the plate than expected, so they pushed the plate over, laughing about the ridiculousness that is North American portion size.

You never turn down chicken wings. You know that by now.

I had never been more grateful for chicken wings. They provided many things. In no order - one, food. Two, conversation. Three, a reduction in weird glances, as it now looked like we were a group of three.

We all got on, bonding a little over being somewhere new and not knowing anyone. After an hour of beers and laughter about "silly Canadian phrases" that the Spaniards didn't understand, we moved to another bar.

A night on the tiles was starting, and stood in the crowd at the next pub was a Canadian husband and wife, Steve and Rachel who were local to Edmonton. They were both in their early fifties. Dressed brightly, they were stoking the party animal flame within them whilst the festival was on.

Steve had just bought a new DSLR camera. He was someone else who foolishly took camera gear to a bar. He'd just bought it, and was still figuring it out, so was rattling off photo after photo, excited by that lovely shutter sound that new Nikon cameras make.

We formed a nifty little group, Steve and Rachel showing us the town. We sat at a table, and over the course of a couple of hours, the drinks flowed. Thoughts of a desperately thinning budget was literally being pissed away.

We passed Steve's camera around, taking photos that would be ghastly to look at in the future. The hours passed, it began to get late.

Rachel went to the bar and came back with a tray full of drinks that we all "had to try." And why the hell wouldn't we.

We barhopped a few more times to new venues. A visceral recollection of one of those, is that of a very sticky dance floor in an Edmonton club. You know it's not going to end well when sticky floors are involved.

Sofia and I got on like a house on fire. After a long time in isolation, and camping at Home bloody Depots, I'd forgotten how to socialise, so made up for it by asking her to become an impromptu Spanish teacher, and attempting to talk solely in

Spanish for the whole night. Which was undoubtedly a cringe-worthy disaster.

Throughout all this time, Claudia had been sat around looking pretty bored. But to be honest, no-one really noticed, as we were all in our own worlds, spurred on by the music and the disturbing stickiness of the floors gluey surface. Our shoes would slowly peel off with a slurp that made 'doing the robot' more effective than ever.

At 3AM we piled out of the bar, all quite slurry. As a group, we had all been quite proudly irresponsible, really embracing the night out. Except Claudia. Damn Claudia.

It's not very cool rocking up at a hosts house at silly o'clock in the morning when you don't know them. Even more so, when they've literally just moved in. So earlier in the night I'd emailed Amie to ask whether her and Alberto wanted to come for a drink, and to let them know that if not, I'd find somewhere to stay in town and return at a more sensible hour.

Where to stay, though, hadn't yet been decided. But life on a bike meant that wasn't a very daunting prospect. It wasn't raining so anywhere was sure to beat Home Depot.

We all mumbled our goodbyes. Off went Rachel and Steve, hand in hand, to a cab. 'Bad Mood Claudia' was in a bad mood. She'd gone off in a tantrum. Sofia and I awkwardly high-fived.

I hazily navigated back to where the bike was locked up, and found a place in the opposite park to fall asleep.

WHERE THE HELL IS MY RUCKSACK?!

At 7AM, that was the thought on my mind. It was nowhere to be seen. A physical 'oh-god-no!' sickness began. Heavy butterflies of dread. How could I have been so stupid?

Making sense of everything was made more difficult by the now raging hangover. "If I can't get this bag back, I have lost everything that has been collected," I muttered. That would be it. No footage. No photos. Forgotten memories.

I'm not trying to exaggerate here, but that rucksack really was the most important non-human thing in my life at that point. There was a priceless amount of sentimental value in that bag. And in my experience, rarely if something goes missing on a night out, does it ever appear again.

What a waste because of a late night at the pub. The damn pub. One other reason why I'd left Manchester the previous year was to escape regular pub culture, a place that had become commonplace at weekends. I had no desire to fall down the common trap of working all week and going to the pub every weekend.

But now, on a very rare return to 'the pub', one of only a small handful of times on the trip, my most important fucking bag had gone missing.

A surge of inspiration and decision pulsed through my veins. I stumbled up from the ground like a newborn deer finding it's balance, and headed straight back to the street where we had been a few hours ago. This was going to take some real Sherlock Holmes savvy.

With fingers crossed, I knocked on the doors to the bars at 9AM. No-one had seen a bag. Searching and searching, nothing was found. A couple of staff members scanned their venues' CCTV footage and saw nothing. There was nothing in the lost and found.

I couldn't think of anything else to do other than go to the police and see if they had any suggestions. With beer breath, I walked in, grass in my hair and clearly looking like I'd just woken up in a park. They asked about the description of the bag, where it might be, and what had happened.

"It could be in one of the bars," I pleaded. "It's black, medium size. Made by F-Stop. A zip on each side. Someone could have taken it. I have no idea, but please help."

The officers were so helpful. They went bar to bar in search of the bag too, but also found nothing. They tapped into CCTV footage, and told me to sit in the reception area of their station and just wait. They'd try to take care of it, this was their job. But they also issued a strong caveat early on, in order to manage expectations.

"It's probable that we'll never find the bag. It's black, just a regular rucksack, hardly stands out from the crowd. The chances are more than slim."

They were working from very little, and after a while, an officer suggested that there was no point staying in the station.

He recommended that I go back to Amie's basement, and they'd get in touch if they found anything.

In despair, I sat on a bench not knowing what to do.

In my pocket was a receipt. It was crumpled, and read '5X BURT REYNOLDS'.

What the hell are BURT REYNOLDS?

It clicked. They were those weird drinks that Rachel had insisted we try. They came with paper mustache stuck on the outside of the glass. And the receipt was from a venue that I'd not searched.

Was this the Golden Ticket? It was time to find out.

Following the address led to the place with the sticky floor. No-one answered the door, it wasn't open yet, but outside was a guy selling artwork on the street called Tim. He knew the owner and called him.

Five minutes later, Frank, the proprietor, opened the door.

"Haha! Ha! Hahaha!" he laughed for such a frustratingly long time, that it seemed like life was being poured away. "Hey, it's you from the group who were obsessed with Burt Reynolds! The Burt Reynolds guy! The mustache guys! Ha! Haaa!"

Someone had left a bag there last night.

"Describe it so I know it's yours and you don't just go round bars stealing stuff," he said, with an ever-present grin.

He marched upstairs, and I felt sick, waiting for his verdict.

It was the bag! It was possible to breathe again.

Never again. NEVER again. I swear.

"You're a lucky git," Tim called from the pavement. He was right. Lucky and idiotic, but the sense of relief was phenomenal.

You can never replace memories.

30

Heaven And Gratitude

SPEEDING DOWNHILL, WHEELS BLURRED WITH VELOCITY, body crouched down into the handlebars. Moments like this were ones of undiluted joy, of rare adrenalin. A more wind resistant posture won't have much of an effect on a bicycle covered in stupidly big pannier bags, but the 'speed crouch' is fun to do, and for a moment you can drift off into an over the top wind-in-hair moment where everything else pales into insignificance.

In my peripheral, a Land Rover was approaching. It slowed down parallel. I was riding on the hard shoulder. There was plenty of room. The passenger window began to wind down. It was probably someone wanting to stop and chat. That happened sometimes.

A half-eaten apple whizzed past my head.

"Haha, you fucker!" the passenger shouted before the Land Rover sped off.

Bicycles rarely work as they're supposed to. Some people enjoy the maintenance and others don't much care for it. Over time, my place in the latter category became more concrete.

The Canadian prairies section was well underway, and it was yet to become totally, completely, unbearably boring, which is what reputation would have you believe. People who talk about flat, long stretches every way you look are lying because it turns out there's plenty of hills in The Prairies, they're just mild and rolling instead of aggressive and steep. Either way, it's a place where you want a range of gears to choose from. Or more than two anyway.

The rear derailleur had broken, ceasing to move the chain onto any other rings than two at the back. Tinkering didn't seem to have much effect, so I crunched along an embarrassingly large portion of Canada, limited to the dual-gears, adamant that there was no need to spend money on repairs if the bike still rolled forwards.

Enough crunch for one day, whilst freewheeling down the street of Lanigan, looking for a suitable patch of grass to collapse on to, a voice called over from the sidewalk.

Teresa Roberts was in her late forties or early fifties, glimmering in the evening sun in a maroon t-shirt, with long brown hair.

"Hey! Going a long way?" she shouted.

10 months to refine the answer to this question meant it was pretty solid. Blindfold me, put me in a barrel, spin me round and throw me off a cliff - it doesn't matter because a response was hardwired and was never going away.

"Oh you must stay! You've finished riding for the day, right?"

I kid you not, Teresa was the owner of a Motel in town, and unlike when Mary and Joseph were kicking it, there was room at the inn.

After piling everything into the available room 8, Teresa and I wandered over to some chairs under a fruit tree in the courtyard to have a chat. And man, was she friendly. That was always the immediate, overwhelming first impression whenever I met people like Teresa - who, if I had to put a label on, would be in the 'soft-spoken and very dedicated Christian' category.

Never had I met anyone quite as enthusiastic about the little things, like the leaves.

"Oh wow. Just wow! Look at those leaves!"

When describing Teresa, it seems like one exclamation mark doesn't quite cut it.

We spoke for a while about the town and how she'd ended up here. She lived with her husband, and she had a couple of now adult kids. We were connecting, and we slowly walked a lap of the grounds. That's when I realised that, in return for staying here, it would be tricky to escape some intense preaching.

"Life is about being focused on Heaven," Teresa exclaimed proudly. "The ultimate trip that we're going to make is to Heaven. So in actual fact, we're not hotel owners. We're travel agents, being able to go out and meet people, and encourage them. Not discuss with them going to Cuba or Hawaii or Saskatchewan, but encourage them to focus on Heaven."

"We're all going to go somewhere when we die. We're going to go to this place, or that place," Teresa held her hands up and pointed in two directions. "There's a choice. The choice is, are we going to go to Heaven or Hell? We want to encourage people to choose Heaven. Choose it now. Start packing your bags for Heaven."

If you spend enough time travelling around North America, you're going to experience this kind of thing. There are more than a small number of people who take pride in showing other people how freakin' rad God is, and who like to build a portfolio of successful converts. But rarely was it quite as explicit as this. Usually it was a slow sell.

"I really think you should turn the rest of your journey into one with a higher purpose," Teresa expressed. "You've not got long left. Keep riding, pray, and put out the good word of God.

Encourage the people you meet to choose Heaven. Dedicate your trip to the Lord."

It was a heartfelt plea.

"Umm. Maybe, I'm still not decided," I replied, but by choosing a noncommittal position, I had accidentally reinforced myself as a target, ripe for being born-again.

God meant everything to Teresa. And part of me agreed with the higher purpose argument. Not in a religious way, but in a meaningful one. It did feel sometimes like the trip had no real purpose. Lots of other people do big trips with a charity angle, they raise money for grand causes. This journey seemed quite selfish in that respect, which wasn't something I was oblivious too. But becoming an affiliate for preaching God was out of the question, for now.

Behind the motel, there was an enormous structure with a waterproof cover over it.

"It's a hot tub," Teresa beamed, "isn't that cool?"

Teresa told the story of how she'd come to own such a thing.

"When you do things in the Lord's name, everything happens for a reason," she explained. "Everything works out. Even if it doesn't seem like it at the time. Like just the other month. I was on Kijiji. I saw that someone was offering to swap a $20,000 hot tub for something. Well, we had an RV that we never used, but it was only worth about $6,000. I thought that there's no way they'll go for the RV without cash on top. But they did! And that's all because of having the Lord's blessing. And similar things have happened for us in real estate too. It's all thanks to the Lord. Now we have a hot tub which we didn't have before, and that's thanks to God. That's why you should finish this journey in the Lord's name."

There's something called 'The Prosperity Gospel', a Christian doctrine. Teresa subscribed to this. It says that financial blessing is the will of God, and that faith to Christian ministries will increase one's material wealth. So I guess the stuff she'd bought could be down to God's blessing, or she could just be really good at finding solid deals online.

It's a tricky one. He doesn't dig materialism, does He? Luke didn't think so. "And He said to them, 'Take care, and be on your guard against all covetousness, for one's life does not consist in the abundance of his possessions.'" (Luke 12:15)

But then know-it-all Matthew throws a spanner in the works, so who knows what to think? "But seek first the kingdom of God and his righteousness, and all these things will be added to you." (Matthew 6:33)

We left the courtyard, calling it a day.

In the morning, the phone in room 8 rang loudly, followed by a knock at the door. Teresa had come to invite me to church. She said that she'd called the Pastor up after our conversation the previous day.

"I really think you'll be interested in what he has to say, he's a very interesting man," she said as I looked at her through newly awoken eyes. "It's just round the corner. I'm leaving in ten minutes. What do you say?"

Thou shalt not lie.

"It's a really kind offer Teresa but I'm feeling a bit under the weather this morning. It's some kind of stomach bug."

And so the tangled web grew. She kept asking questions and I kept spitting out excuses, struggling to drum up the motivation to be preached to again.

"Oh, I'm sorry to hear that. I'll tell you what," Teresa said, "you stay here another night. Take the day off, sleep here again tonight, and hopefully this time tomorrow you'll be recovered. I'll just see if the Pastor is willing to come and meet you here tomorrow morning instead."

I went back to bed. The pressure was less there. It seemed like only moments had passed. Until. Knock, knock. Who's there? Teresa at the door of room 8 again. She'd just come back from service. A couple of hours had passed and she wanted to check in, to see how the stomach bug was doing.

"How are you feeling?" she asked, and at first I had no idea what she was talking about, until quickly remembering I was supposed to be sick.

"Oh, still not great," I mumbled pathetically, like a seven year old who wants the day off school.

She put out her hands, and in it was a foil-wrapped plate. "Just a little something from church to make you feel better."

It was a plate full of 5 pancakes, syrup, banana, bacon. Like something you'd eat in Heaven.

Time was getting on, and in the grand scheme of things, it was chilly and only getting chillier. So the next morning, it truly was time to go.

I peeked out of the window and saw Teresa. She was with someone in the courtyard. Could it be the Pastor?

We've all seen the movies. Die Hard, for example. So like you, I know to look for a grill in the ceiling which I can unscrew, shimmy into and along, drop through an air-shoot into an adjacent motel room complete with a clever comment like "Oh hey, just dropping in," and then pedal smoothly off into the distance, avoiding Teresa and the Pastor's heavy preaching at all costs. But there is no grill, I'm trapped. Plus, lifting a heavy bike into a ventilation system to escape an awkward conversation seems like a lot of work. Oh, and I ought to give her back the plate on which she kindly delivered the surprise breakfast.

I rotated room 8's door knob, and the sun rushed in. Walking over to Teresa and the Pastor with my helmet on, I hoped it would indicate some kind of rush and necessity to leave.

"You must be Dave," Pastor Rob guessed.

You can imagine what followed. It was an uncomfortable forty-five minutes about all the benefits of our Creator.

"I know it all sounds whacky, but try it," insisted Rob. "You will feel very different and have a real, true sense of purpose in life."

It would be nice to believe it all. It's more than simply an issue of purpose and friendliness - the religious people I've met seem so thankful. They seem look at life differently, and literally thank God for every little joy, at least on the surface - every bite of food, sip of water, sunny day, even a bargain hot tub or some leaves. They seem more thankful for life itself than most people. More appreciative for the unlikely and miraculous fact that we exist at all. Maybe that's a trait we'd all be wise to carry, regardless of our views.

Sometimes it's good to be reminded of being grateful now, because in a minute or an hour or a day it could all be very different. Maybe an unexpected asteroid would kill us all, or there'd be an email from home about a loved one getting ill. Everything could change as quickly as a snap of the fingers.

Coincidentally it says as much in the Bible, when it advises "Do not boast about tomorrow, for you do not know what a day may bring forth" (Proverbs 27:1)

Meeting Teresa reminded me that gratitude is not random. It's a practice, it's conscious. And as long as we're living and breathing, we have a lot to be thankful for.

That said, another lame and pathetic excuse later, I pedalled away, clunking down the road in the only two gears that worked properly, progressing once again along The Prairies. Yet to be born-again, but reminded of a valuable lesson.

31

Connection And
Stench

WHEN YOU'RE NOT GOING INSANE, YOU CAN APPRECIATE the little things because there is nothing else. Just empty roads, insane sunset glows, roaring thunderstorms, natural elements.

"This is as natural as you get it!" Brad had once screamed jubilantly, several months before this. He was right. At times, this was the good life.

Every day, Mother Nature showed herself. Being outside for a long time makes you witness something that can be lost when office life takes over. The seasons progress, and you actually see it happening in front of your eyes. The colours, air, and temperature shifts. Never before had I witnessed seasons change like this.

Winnipeg, Manitoba is really close to the longitudinal centre of North America, basically slap bang in the centre of Canada. It's a city of 660,000 people, it's where Winnie The Pooh was created, and in winter the temperature can drop to -40 Celsius without taking windchill into account. Winnipeg stood out as a marker. The first time when the incoming winter seemed close.

It was October, and two locals both said something that carried the same message.

"There's still a long way to go, you'd better get a move on! When the first snowfall comes, that's usually it for the rest of the winter. It could be anywhere from 2 weeks to 6 weeks from now, but if you're riding across the country you should try to get as far away as possible!"

So by all accounts, Winnipeg gets nippy. Dangerously and properly nippy, not put-on-another-fleece nippy.

There was an atmosphere in the city, the kind that meant something special was happening. Posters plastered in alcoves, and on billboards and lampposts in the city, pointed to an event. There was a music show on in a couple of days, and Sierra Noble was performing. I'd never heard of her, but people seemed excited and the gig was supposedly a bit of a homecoming.

By utter coincidence, a local called Matt, who I bumped into at a post office, was one of the gig organisers. He explained that the night was the "Concert For Peace," an event that coincides with The International Day of Peace, an annual 24 hour window that the UN has devoted to strengthening the ideals of peace around the world. He mentioned that they'd been working on it for ages.

"Come down, it's going to be great!" he beamed.

Sierra and I spoke by email and arranged to meet a couple of days later to do a bit of filming. She was one of Canada's leading fiddle players, and had recently established herself as a singer-songwriter, once supporting some dude called Bon Jovi. Who? I'd never heard of him either. When she was 13, she started touring across the world, and for the last decade has never really stopped moving. Perhaps there are parallels, albeit slight ones, between being a musician and travelling by bicycle. A tenuous link to movement.

Sierra sang an outdoor session to provide the backdrop to our little makeshift film. I asked her some questions in between songs. What wisdom was in her brain?

"I guess I went through a little bit of a period when I was younger," she said in a soft-spoken voice, "of wishing that I could've had a normal teenage life, which I didn't have at all, because I was on tour all the time. But that was my normal, and looking back on it, I wouldn't trade a single thing to go to one party on a weekend. It's been such a blessing."

It's easy to feel out of place when we compare ourselves to others. Sometimes we look across and see people who, from our point of view, look like they have everything figured out, who've found their calling. But this can be a naive mindset to have, because often our assumptions are unfounded and we don't consider the trying times of self-doubt that all people have. But in rare cases, maybe things do click.

"I remember the first time that my violin teacher put a violin in my arms," Sierra recalled, "and looking back on it, what I remember is I felt whole. I guess you can say, from that moment I found my calling. I always knew what it was. I was someone who did really know who I was at a very young age, and what I wanted to do in life. People tried to tell me that wasn't cool or it wasn't acceptable, and it really got to me for a long time. But I kept going... I think the most important thing that anybody needs to hear at any point in life, is 'it's okay to be who you are.'"

"Honestly, not thinking about it is the best thing you can do," Sierra advised on what someone should do if they're a little lost, "and staying open - keeping your heart and mind open. And if you're even this much drawn to something, go in that direction, check it out, go through the door, check out the room. If it's cool sit in it for 5 minutes. Be like 'what's gonna happen? I don't know. Oh nothing happened, next door!'"

How do you find inspiration when it seems thin on the ground?

"I find that I get the most stuck when I think about it too much. It's the same with writers block and all that. People rack their brains for inspiration, when that's not where you find inspiration. Inspiration isn't often in our brains, it's around us, and we have to just stop and listen to the universe."

When you move a lot, you miss people, and you feel isolated and crazy because of spending too much time in your own head. But some tricks can be picked up to counter this. Happiness hacks. Sierra had come upon this too, and had developed some techniques.

"I think that it's those times where you're having a bad day and you're tired and you look in the mirror and it's just like 'I look like crap, I feel horrible, I'm exhausted, I don't feel like doing the show...' It's really easy to convince yourself that you feel alone and tired of all of it, but it's also really easy to open yourself up to connecting with people anywhere, and it doesn't have to be anyone that you know. It can be a 10 second genuine exchange with a human being, that can completely recharge your being."

"I've realized that life is really fulfilled by connection," she continued, "and humans thrive in connection. And if we cut ourselves off, whether it be our own doing or whether we're cut off by other reasons, that's when we stop thriving."

We stopped recording and Sierra went to start rehearsals. It had been refreshing to talk to someone who understood the mind-mess that being on the move can be. There can be a darkness attached to movement, and it was valuable to be reminded of connection as a remedy. Throughout the previous months on the road, I'd unconsciously learnt this too. The great times were often those that involved shared experiences. And the dark times, those happened in times of isolation.

The concert was great, although one of the acts was a rapping duo whose lyrics revolved around peace for all. Which was weird, because everyone knows hip-hop should be about private jets, bling, guns and strippers, not joy and togetherness. Nonetheless, it was inspiring to be in a huge concert hall full of people from all walks of life coming together to celebrate peace - a theme that, if you absorb world news even a little bit, can seem to be rare. Which, in reality, isn't the case at all.

Places, and memories of good times, have little to do with the sights or the architecture or activities or anything like that. All of that is trivial. Places earn fond memories because of the people in them and the connections made. That's the reason some places had been a struggle, and others had been joyful.

A few days later, I rode out of the city with a smile. Pedalling into the night, sweating lightly and falling back into routine, I glanced over to the left and looked into the sky.

There it was, glowing with green and purple pulses. A tingle overtook the air. I pulled over to the side of the road to look properly. The Northern Lights were on display. What a sight. Absolutely magical.

Jubilations were cut short later, though, when a shopkeeper exclaimed, "You know you smell, right?"as I handed him a loaf of bread over the counter.

He proceeded to tell the story of when he lived in Iraq and took a bus for 72 hours straight and smelt really bad by the end of it too.

"I understand what it's like," he sympathised.

Nothing like peaceful human connection to let you know that you stink.

32

Yapping And Fun

Lake Superior is beautiful and never-ending, stretching as far as the eye can see, like the biggest ocean.

After the Northern Lights sighting, I'd been slowly cycling towards Thunder Bay, a city in Western Ontario, at the head of Lake Superior. As cities go, it was quite new, being formed in 1970 after a merger of two former cities and two former towns - Fort William, Port Arthur, Neebing and McIntyre. At the time, local residents were given a vote, with a shortlist of new names, 'Thunder Bay', 'Lakehead' and 'The Lakehead', the former coming out on top. A good decision I reckon because Thunder Bay sounds way cooler than the others.

The Canadian Prairies ended in Manitoba. They were over. It had taken a long time, 7 weeks all in all to get through 'the flats', and now that they were complete, I felt qualified to have an opinion when it concerned the dull, shoot-yourself-in-the-face-because-it's-so-boring reputation that The Prairies have.

Firstly, as I mentioned earlier, anyone who says "The Prairies are flat" is lying. There's plenty of hills. Secondly, there are of course stretches which are dull and samey, but no more than many other places.

Something that is challenging to get used to, when doing anything for a long time, is that it's not always going to be fun. Big projects are often more of a mental game than anything else, which is something that it's wise to embrace, because they'll be the fondest memories with time, even though they might, sometimes, drive you round the bend and make you want to scream.

Here's a scale created by Kelly Cordes, an American alpinist: Type 1 fun - smiley and brilliant. Type 2 fun - horrible at the time but you'll look back on it and remember it as being fun. Type 3 fun - no fun at all, ever. Large projects of any kind, and certainly long bicycle journeys, come with plenty of Type 2.

It took 10 days to cycle the 438 miles between Winnipeg and Thunder Bay. With each night came an impending clarity that the jaws of the approaching winter were not far behind. They were yapping at my heels. It wasn't snowy yet, but to be relatively comfortable in the tent meant wearing almost every clothing item that I was carrying, and even this resulted in nights spent shivering away, teeth chattering like a naked Inuit with a broken hot water bottle.

The thought of sourcing a warmer sleeping bag was top of mind. However, each time I looked at a map of North America, the end of the journey was relatively in sight. So much so, that I was now confident enough in the specific end time of the trip, and had a date to work to. Surely there was no need to get any new gear now, in these last few weeks. How cold could it get, anyway?

Mechanical issues were still ongoing too. The same clunky two-gear setup that I'd been rocking for a while remained. Sometimes I forgot about it, quite content and thinking everything was fine, until I pushed hard on the gear shifter and there'd be a fierce metal-on-metal rubbing noise, worse than nails on a chalkboard.

The realisation that fixing the bike was an important part of making these last few weeks go smoothly became clear, of course. Why the hell did it take so long? The truth is, I think I possibly have a deep desire to make things difficult, and get a sense of twisted pride from that, thinking things like 'getting cold each night makes me a better person'. Or an idiot, either one. But as oddly personified as it may sound, I felt the bike deserved to finish the journey with grace, not haggard like a elderly 50-a-day smoker with lung problems.

A bike shop in Thunder Bay fixed the gear issue. In fact they made the dark magic that is derailleur maintenance look easy. To the point where it was ridiculous how quickly they managed to fix it. Under three minutes, and the complete range of gears were back in action. Which was quite embarrassing, to be honest.

Vanished were the rolling hills of The Prairies, to be replaced with the first brutally steep climbs in a long while. The last time they were quite as aggressive was British Columbia. Steep tough uphills, real physical work that led to a pounding heart, followed by the ever-gratifying reward of gravity and a steep descent. Over and over again, at the top of each climb was the never-ending sight of the lake.

You hear them before you see them.

Dogs.

There's plenty of horror stories among bicycle travellers of dog attacks. Kentucky seems to be a particularly renowned area. Chases are common, and there's something quite off-putting about hearing an aggressive bark but not yet seeing the beast. Usually it's a friendly, tiny, inquisitive dog that loves the chase. Only rarely is it of any concern.

If the dog in question does look aggressive, a system of getting off the bike and standing still always works. The dog gets bored after a few seconds and retreats. Sometimes they lie down and roll around, looking to be stroked, which is hardly the stuff of nightmares.

Above Lake Superior, there were three Pit Bull's. The moment probably only lasted two minutes, although it seemed like sixty seven years. These were not small or friendly. Rather than curious, they were aggressive. And they wore identical heavy-metal chainring collars, with matching foaming mouths.

They ran out from a timber yard. The perfect guard dogs, any would-be timber thieves would be in for a nasty surprise. As they charged over, the noise came first, as it always did. Three blurry figures in my peripheral. Then a realisation that these dogs might not lie down and roll around. No. No they wouldn't. Definitely not. That was clear now.

I slammed on the brakes, jumped off the bike and stood behind it, fashioning a bicycle-shaped shield.

"NO! NO! AWAY! AWAY! AWAY NOW!" at the beginning of the trip, someone with Kentucky-experience had told me to shout in a commanding way at any violent-looking dogs. Be authoritative.

They were now just standing there, barking with a ferocious, drooling roar a couple of feet away. The commands, no matter the level of authoritativeness, didn't do anything. Maybe a better strategy would've been to pedal as hard as possible and attempt to outrun them. The bike had gears now, after all. But the hounds looked fast.

They were in a pack, huddled together like the front row of a scrum. They continued to roar. It sounded much more like roaring than barking.

One of them opened their jaws to strike. It did not go for me, it didn't want flesh. Perhaps it was the smell of peanut butter, but it struck out like a king cobra towards the bright red rear pannier bag, as the other two stood by and continued to snarl.

The road had been quiet that morning, but thankfully, whilst pushing the bike back and forth and attempting to dissuade the dogs, and continuing to shout "NO! AWAY!" three cars drove onto the scene. The car at the front saw what was going on and stopped. The driver took to the car horn.

Honk, honk, honk.

The drivers behind this one were either irritated that there was now a traffic jam, or they also saw the scene, as suddenly three cars were horning loudly. Suddenly the solitude that surrounded Lake Superior had become as loud as Istanbul at rush hour.

The noise did nothing to distract the dogs. But there was comfort in knowing that if they became ravenous, there were people around who might offer help, or a ride to the hospital.

The horns drew the attention of someone from the timber yard. He ran over, and called out as only an owner can. The dogs retreated, away from the road and back to their guard dog positions.

"Sorry about that!" the man shouted, before returning to work.

"Oh, it's all good!" I replied.

Hopefully the shaking wasn't too visible.

33

Baby It's Cold Outside

"WHEN THE FIRST SNOWFALL COMES, THAT'S USUALLY IT for the rest of the winter."

The Winnipeg resident's advice echoed at the forefront of my mind as heavy, sticky snow fell to the ground in Sault Ste. Marie, on the Eastern side of Lake Superior.

The falling powder, low visibility and the Baltic chill all showed no immediate signs of letting up. It was going to be a glove day, once I'd drummed up enough motivation to face the elements.

There was no real reason to not be motivated, as I'd spent the night in a motel. So it hadn't been a hardcore, cold night, and there had been no suffering. But opening the door and being hit by the chill was a shock, even after all this time experiencing gradual seasonal change.

The cold was enough of a reason to close the door, rustle around in the pannier bags, and find more layers. Of which, there were no more.

After leaving the room and setting out, I rode for twenty minutes. Along the snowy pavements, with the rain jacket hood done up tight over the shell of my helmet. It was a balancing act, performed at a slow pace. In the snow, it would be easy to turn too sharply, fall and slide along the whiteness, especially with balding tyres.

Riding took focus, which was rare. Cars would drive by, their lights bright to tackle the fog, and spray would fire up from their wheels to land on the pavement. Offsets of that spray would hit the few exposed parts of my face that were left, and every time a shiver would run down my spine as though someone had poured ice cubes down my shirt and run away giggling.

It was clear that it wasn't a smooth start to the day, and acting on those initial signs had become a bit of a superstition.

The familiar red logo, and the cars in the drive through lane - that would be a good place to drum up motivation. A familiar place, a warm place. A place that, if visited too much, makes you feel guilty that you're not truly living the 'adventurous nature' of a trip like this. But the roast beef sandwich combo at Tim Hortons would warm me up, and for a brief while there would be no guilt. There was motivation inside those four walls, there was time to get fired up.

It was the end of October, and whoever was in charge of Tim's music selection had decided that they would try to en-courage some early Christmas spirit, by playing songs to match the fresh Lapland-esque scene that was now on display outside the window. One in particular, struck a chord that day. "Baby It's Cold Outside." Whoever penned that song must've cycled a long way at some point.

Within the confines of Tim's hospitality, the lyrics, whilst corny, seemed to sum up exactly, word for word, what was running through my head. They represented an internal mono-logue, of brain versus body.

{I really can't stay} - There was a narrow window of time left to reach the end of the journey.

{But baby it's cold outside} - It really was.

{I've got to go away} - Time was a fuse.

{But baby it's cold outside} - The roast beef combo was looking up from the plate like a mindreader.

The realisation that I hadn't set out on this journey to sit in a Tim Hortons didn't take long to reach. It was time to go. 'Man up you big pansy' - the internal monologue would say, an anti-pathetic alarm.

Once I'd put every layer back on and wrapped a doubled up bin bag around the leather saddle on the bike, I finally set off, still precariously rolling along the snow-filled sidewalks. The spray that was being kicked up from the bicycle made me long for the wheel fenders that were now long gone, left behind, as in the summer they had seemed completely obsolete.

It's still a sweaty game, regardless of the cold. Sweaty enough for a shirt to become damp at any rate.

When it began to get dark, the landscape turned remote, in the kind of way that would be perfect, were the ground not reminiscent of a scene from The Snowman. There was plenty of land, and most land owners would surely be tucked up in their living room for the night. What's not to like about that kind of sleep-anywhere freedom?

Pedalling towards the horizon, scanning the farmland, it seemed like there were a couple of options. One was to pitch in a field - maybe in the corner of one it would be possible to find some sort of shield from the elements. Another was to find somewhere that was sheltered. The latter would be good tonight, as it was clearly going to be one hell of a cold night, the coldest so far. Both water bottles were now frozen solid, silently attached to the bike frame instead of the normal loud sloshing.

What was that? It looked like a barn. It was. Far ahead, slightly off to the side of the road, there was a wooden barn with a green roof. It had three walls, open at one side.

As it was still a distance away, there were a few minutes of cycling time to consider a) whether sleeping in a barn was trespassing and b) because it clearly was trespassing, whether I was willing to trespass for the benefits of shelter.

Another question of morality, there had been a few. I'd done enough trespassing on private land, so that didn't cause any real internal concern, but this felt a little different because a barn is actual shelter, it's not like sleeping in the corner of a field. To make a decision became an internal role-play exercise. Brain versus body again.

If I was a farmer, and it was freezing outside, would I care if someone camped in my barn? The answer was: no, not really, as long as they didn't burn the place down or steal anything.

And so the decision was made, and I headed to the barn, finding that inside sat a bright orange Hesston combine harvester and some miscellaneous heavy-duty farming machinery. The ground was dry, the roof was solid. It was still going to be one hell of a cold night, but it would be a sheltered one, at least on three sides.

You know when you just can't get a song out of your head? The second verse of that song was running over and over, a guilty pleasure on an internal loop, impossible to drown out, as the dusk disappeared and nightfall arrived.

{This evening has been}
{Been hoping that you'd drop in.}
{So very nice}
{I'll hold your hands. They're just like ice.}

Nestled in the space between the machinery, shivering as my hands were sandwiched tight under each armpit, the words seemed appropriate. Just like ice.

Surely it had been a foolish decision to not upgrade to warmer sleeping kit, even if it would only make these last few weeks more comfortable, and nothing more? But going back to my twisted sense of achievement under trying conditions, enduring these nights seemed like a challenge worth taking on. Maybe it was because it was these kind of shivering moments, that didn't involve motels or Christmas music or roast beef sandwiches, that were the ones, deep down, that I'd been looking for. On a continent where it can seem like ease and comfort is never too far away, there is value in these moments of relative suffering and isolation.

With only a couple of weeks of this way of life left, the barn provided the most 'just stay alive until the morning' kind of night. I tried to think back to any similar times. There'd been plenty of freezing nights, plenty of solid water bottles, but nothing quite like this.

It can be easy to lose track of time when days and weeks blend together, like they do when a project goes on for a long time. Time, in general, becomes a blur. When I woke up in that barn the following morning, and touched the merino wool shirt which had become rock hard in the night as the sweat froze, the cyclical nature of this journey, and of long journeys as a whole, became apparent.

The bike ride had gone through every season, each one bringing challenges and opportunities. And I'm not going to pretend that waking up in the barn to a frozen shirt was a particularly pleasant one, because it wasn't at all, but it was worth it.

Winter 2012 to winter 2013. Four seasons ticked off, like simple boxes on a questionnaire. That full-circle had made the trip more vast and worthwhile than it was ever first imagined to be. Sometimes it can be worthwhile to stubbornly grit your way through things, even if it, at times, they may seem 'too much'.

Cursing the shirt, and then smiling at the meta-significance of it, there was no doubt at all that, one day, I'd look back on that night as a special one.

34

Death And Axes

IN SUDBURY, TIME WAS RUNNING OUT AND IT SEEMED LIKE there was one priority left. Ego made me view crossing the 'finish line' by bike as the only option worth considering. It would really suck to ride for another week and then end up taking public transport into New York City to get to the airport on time. With a year invested, something seemed wrong with that.

So I booked a train ticket from Sudbury to Toronto to ensure finishing by pedal-power. It was 9PM. The train wouldn't set off until later, due at 1.30AM.

The station was located on the outskirts of town. In the darkness, I rode in the general direction of 'Sudbury Junction', rolling vaguely towards it amongst the bare trees that took up any space not taken by a building or a road. To the left was a coffee shop that looked warm. The bright lights from inside spilled out onto the concrete, acting as a tractor beam, and enticing me in.

"Are you travelling somewhere?" a man asked, also on his way inside from the sidewalk.

There hadn't been many long conversations recently, and with enough time in silence, an inevitable sense of stir craziness had started to rear it's ugly head. Conversations after a long time with none took some warming up to get into again.

Barry explained that he'd been retired for several years, and had been a Sudbury resident for his entire life. In his early twenties, he'd spent 10 days hitchhiking around the Great Lakes, and since then had never left his hometown. He'd settled down with his wife Brenda, "a city girl at heart." Describing her with a loving smile, he said "she doesn't like travelling, so I've never been anywhere since that original road trip."

I asked him whether he wanted to travel anywhere in the future.

"Sometimes when I spot hitchhikers and travellers on the road," he said, "I pick them up and talk to them about their travels and the places they've been. I love the idea of travelling, but I'm content to travel vicariously through other people's trips. That's fine by me. Fresh air is the same everywhere, right? So I'm happy to experience new places using the computer."

Anyone drawn to travel may see flaws in this, but I think there's something quite special about thinking like that. Contentment. Maybe a lot of us who travel around do so because we are unsettled. Maybe, in some ways, being as content as Barry is the very thing that many of us are looking for. If you can be happy at home, as part of a community, then that is something to be proud of.

I admitted to Barry that settling down (ideally with Taylor Swift) and building a home is something I definitely aspire to, if life works out that way, and that living a life on the road forever certainly wasn't the grand plan!

After a coffee and a donut, Barry asked if he could drive me to the train station. "It's far away and hard to find. And it's freezing out there," he said with a tone of concern.

Sometimes it seemed as though people saw the bike, and the gear, and the darkness, and then felt an urge to go out of their way to offer help in a kind of surrogate-parent way. And when this was the case, turning down their help could a) appear insulting and b) mean missing out on friendships formed.

We walked outside, unlocked the bike, and began strolling to Barry's house where his truck was parked. When it happens, it happens fast, and is never subtle. The God-is-great vibe. Barry asked about my beliefs, and I reverted to the classic fall back answer in times like this.

"Oh, I've not decided yet. It's all a bit cloudy to be honest."

Never sit on the fence. Sitting on the fence gets a nod and then an explanation as to why God is awesome and why He is the answer to everyone's problems. But that didn't really happen on the walk with Barry.

Instead, as we walked and talked, Barry threw a real curve-ball, shifting the topic to something that seemed only loosely related, and as he said it I became increasingly aware of the bear spray and where it was, if it needed to be reached quickly.

"You know Dave? I scared my daughter's boyfriend a few months back," he said, in a quiet and unassuming voice. "We watched a movie, and the main character is sent a message from God that he has to remove some evil souls from the Earth. One day he's driving along a country lane and sees a beam of light on a barn. He goes in, and the light is shining on an axe."

For a moment, I was immediately regretting taking a casual walk with Barry. It was late. We were strangers. I could see why his daughters boyfriend was scared. Barry was hardly describing Mr Bean, was he?

Was this a clue that he had an axe ready at his house? And perhaps in the basement were bodies of pickaxed hitchhikers that he'd lured home. In Barry's eyes, was I an evil soul that he'd been instructed by God to remove from the Earth? Hopefully not, that would suck.

"He proceeds to kill various people," Barry went on to explain, "by chopping them up into little pieces. At the end, you see what they've done. One of the victims was a pervert and did things with young children, another smothered a disabled person with a cushion. They'd all done bad things, and this man was just doing what God asked him to."

Oki doke.

Halloween was in a couple of days. It all got pretty scary suddenly and I felt nervous. I looked at him with a serious questioning face, trying to weigh up whether this was unusual humour or something to actually be concerned about. He looked back with a blank expression, not doing much to calm my anxiety. Until a brief moment later, where his serious face converted to a beaming practical-joker smile.

"Oh, I'm not scaring you am I?" he laughed deeply. "I'm not a axe murderer, don't worry. Although I could be. You've just met me. I could be putting on a front and be luring you back to my house. Or you could be a murderer. It's hard to tell."

We continued to walk and my heartbeat began to slow a little. Everything became light-hearted again, and we laughed as we proceeded to his house.

Barry explained how he'd injured his leg recently and he liked to walk as much as possible to rebuild the muscles. When we arrived at his home, half an hour after setting out from the coffee shop, I briefly met Brenda, Barry's wife. She was lovely, and it immediately clicked that this was the house of two friendly retirees who were dedicated to their church. They were not axe-murderers, which was a relief.

We made small talk before leaving the house, cramming everything into Barry's truck, and setting off on the short journey towards Sudbury Junction.

In between the camping by the side of the road, and generally the days becoming a blur, these kind of nights and moments of kindness really stand out. The station was hidden down a discreet lane and would've been hard to find without local knowledge, so as we parted I thanked Barry for all the generosity.

We stepped out of the truck and he fetched a bag. There was still a very slim chance that his lovely wife Brenda had been a well acted cover story, and inside the bag was going to be a swing of an axe to the temple.

"I really hope you enjoy this and get a chance to read the book."

Barry handed over a copy of the New Testament, and a massive bag of sandwiches and chocolate for the train ride. And once again, a strangers kindness was remarkable.

The train was delayed until 3.30AM.

Sitting in the waiting room and ploughing down the food that Barry and Brenda had provided, I began flicking through the New Testament. All the religious people I'd met had shown amazing generosity. Maybe this book is what caused their optimistic zest for life. It was worth a punt.

The train pulled in to the station. Helped by the station manager, Tom, we lifted the bike into the luggage car. I walked to find the reserved seat, sat down, and was out like a light.

35

Random Acts Of Kindness

T HE RAIN WAS BATTERING DOWN ON THE TENT, WHICH WAS pitched 10ft away from the road, poorly hidden in between a single tree and a wooden fence.

Thud, thud, thud. As the liquid fell from the sky, the shifting shadows of the droplets on the material was a gateway to a weird trance. Several minutes of just staring at them rolling down. A cloudy mind because this would all be over soon, and that was hard to make sense of.

Outside, the bicycle was getting drenched. Hopefully the makeshift saddle cover had done its job, however I doubted that the front puncture had mended itself in the night.

These moments would be missed, and the mental haze of an impending finish, crossed with the thought of stepping back to normality, was more stressful than being inside the tent. The waterproof walls had been home for a long time now. Not a comfortable one, but home nonetheless.

The pool of water that had formed around the groundsheet turned my dwelling into an island of comfort, floating in a sea of not knowing what to think. From the relative warmth of the sleeping bag, I glanced over at my phone. Condensation had built up on the screen, making it wet and blurry. The phone had been switched on Airplane Mode for the last 11 months, and was now just a clock, note-keeping device, and music player. Wiping the surface revealed a new day. 08.15, Thursday 31st October. Halloween.

Mornings like this began in the same way. You wait... Wait... Wait a bit more... You hope that the rain stops, and in that brief weather window you become a packing-ninja, putting everything back in the pannier bags with lightning speed before everything becomes soaked. A skill, no, an intuition, that is finely developed over time, and regularly fails miserably.

Eventually, after the initial optimism that 'yep, it will definitely dry up soon', you begin to realise that it's now or never. On go the waterproofs, you crawl outside, you accidentally kneel in mud, end up somehow getting soaked and cold, and a few minutes later everything is packed and you're ready to move on.

Another day, another puncture. Pushing the bike into Bronte Village, a small fishing community on the shore of Lake Ontario, I found shelter under a bus stop to fix it. As well as becoming a packing-ninja, it was occasionally necessary to become a shelter-finding ninja, too.

On closer inspection, this wasn't just a puncture, it was a massive hole right through the tyre.

Bronte Village is a very affluent place, and the bike shop in the village was high end, with carbon fibre road bikes and ultra lightweight racing gear built for triathletes. It was a place that would make most dirty and broke touring cyclists quiver in their boots, because they usually aren't in the market for a $7000 bike. The shop didn't have any 700cc tyres, which was irritating.

"Do you have any duct tape?" I asked.

The manager laughed and nodded when she realised what that question meant. Most people came in and put their bike in for repair or left with shiny new gear, they clearly didn't get many people asking for some tape to stick a dodgy tyre together.

"Give me a minute." She headed back into the workshop and came out minutes later, carrying a roll of tape. "Have this," she smiled. "Hopefully it gets you to where you're going."

Back under the bus stop, I taped the inside of the split, slotted a new inner tube inside, twisted the bead of the tyre back onto the rim, and pumped up the tube cautiously. I'd caused a panic once, months earlier, by being responsible for an exploding inner tube that sounded suspiciously like a gunshot in El Paso, and I didn't want to do the same here.

As the tube inflated with air, the split became a little more pronounced. When the gauge on the pump read 70 PSI, the tape remained in position, covering the split. A ghetto bodge.

Near Hamilton, a city on the Western point of Lake Ontario, daylight fell and groups of children flocked to the street. Suddenly the scene changed, and I cycled through what appeared to be the set from 28 Days Later. Ghosts, zombies, pumpkins and pirates began to fill the streets, armed with empty buckets that would soon be full of candy.

Relentless downpours have a way of finding gaps, and even if that's not what does it, sweat build up inside your waterproof provides a guarantee that, one way or the other, becoming drenched is the order of the night.

It was getting late. There must be an escape, somewhere with a heater, and hot drinks. Somewhere to hide before building my tent-based home and going to sleep. You know where I'm going with this. Tim Hortons. My second home. A place where it's easy to while away the hours, and to let time pass you by.

I rode to the nearest glowing Tim's logo, and piled inside, to the nearest table in order to escape the incessant downpour. I sat and became lost in cloudy thought. Snapping out of it, and looking down to check the time again, it had somehow become 02.07AM, Friday 1st November.

There were a couple of things that were unusual about this situation. One, it was November. Crikey. I'd set off in November the previous year, so it marked 12 months of doing this, which was probably apparent in the bags under my eyes. Two, IT WAS 2 IN THE MORNING and I was sat alone in the corner of a Tim Hortons.

Two other people each occupied a table across the room. Both had their head in their hands, their hoods tightly strung, asleep. This was an eye opener, a hack for when necessary, because the few staff members behind the counter didn't seem to care that the place had turned into a makeshift hostel.

Those two knights of the night sparked some inspiration. Sleeping here seemed like a far better option than going out into the downpour and spending time finding a place to set up. Especially now, at two in the morning. So why the hell not. Head on the table, I slept.

At 6AM, Tim's began to get populated with early morning workers. I messily wiped the drool that had built up in the night and saw that the knights of the night had now left.

Outside was dry again - dry! Moving. Settling back into the zone, the meditative state where worries vanish and you are present. The duct tape bodge was still holding the tyre together. It made a crunching, rippling noise on each revolution, which was accompanied with a physical bump that echoed down the entire frame and provided jolts on each spin. Definitely not a long term solution, but that was okay because Niagara Falls was the end goal for the day, and on dry roads, 49 miles away shouldn't be any trouble.

BANG! The loudest puncture I've ever heard, and an instant flat tyre. They probably heard this one in El Paso too. The tube had an enormous hole in it, located on the very same part as the gaping split in the tyre. You could've fitted a golf ball through it. It was really annoying, but buried in a bag somewhere was the roll of tape and another inner tube. And Niagara wasn't too far away now. So I could do another bodge here, and then find a new tyre there. Problem solved.

I replaced the tatty tape, slotted in another new inner tube, nervously pumped it up again, and rode off.

30 metres. I'm not kidding. 30 bloody metres.

BANG!

You cannot be serious. One step in front of the other, I changed from cleats to trainers and began pushing the bike in the direction of Niagara Falls. Walking for a couple of hours, I became lost in hip-hop that was about real issues, like pimps and dealin', not togetherness and joy like in Winnipeg.

A car approached. After a few seconds, it was parallel to me, driving along at a matched pace. The window opened and a friendly face appeared from the far side of the vehicle, shouting over with the positivity of Ned Flanders. "Seems like you have a problem! Where are you heading?"

"It's just a puncture, nothing serious," I shouted back, "I'm heading to Niagara Falls and will get it fixed there."

"Want a lift? I live in Niagara and am driving back now. I'm a cyclist too!"

Mike was an accountant who lived with his high-school-crush-turned-wife, Heather, in Niagara Falls.

"You know, this is such a bizarre coincidence," Mike laughed. "I hardly ever drive home from work. And on the very rare occasions that I do, I never take this route! And just last night, I took out the rear seats in the car to free up space for work!"

Seemed like fate, which was a theme that came up a lot.

Mike invited me in to his home for dinner and to meet Heather. We pulled into the leafy street that he lived on, and went inside.

Heather was a nurse. She and Mike had 4 kids, now adults, who mostly lived locally. Mike's mother had recently moved in to the house, and was British. The crazy thing was, she used to live in Workington, a really small, obscure rural town about 45 miles away from my hometown. A very small world moment.

We all got on really well. We ate pizza and joked. These moments made the memories.

"Do you want to stay?" Heather asked, "we have a spare room downstairs, right next to all of Mike's bikes."

Heather was working a night shift at the hospital, so we piled into the car to drop her off. Mike suggested I tag along so he could show me around Niagara Falls from the Canadian side. The enormous Niagara River provides a natural split between Canada and the United States.

At night the falls were lit up, a mystical myriad of shifting colours being beamed onto the water from the edge via projection. It was a commercial marketing gimmick to encourage photographs and designed to wow tourists, but flipping heck, it didn't half work. The falls are quite a sight, absolutely massive at 165 feet tall. A woman called Annie Edson Taylor went over them in a wooden barrel once as a publicity stunt. The first person to ever survive the drop, way back in 1901. Which is absolutely mental.

Back at Heather and Mike's, I woke up the next morning and stumbled upstairs into the dining room. In a culinary parallel to the falls, it was a remarkable breakfast spread. Pancakes, waffles, syrups, fruit salad, cereal. And like Annie, I hoped to survive said breakfast.

Mike walked into the house to join us, and went to the sink in order to wash his oddly oily hands.

"Oh, I hope you don't mind," he said, as he sat down and began digging in, "but I've been in the garage fixing your bike. I oiled it and replaced the front tyre with one I had lying around. Is that okay?"

Mike and Heather were total heroes with hearts of gold. And after breakfast I carted all the pannier bags outside and started to pack the bike, to find that he'd even cleaned the damn thing!

Time to get going. Heather came out, carrying a newspaper. "So this made me laugh," she said. "We had no idea, but apparently yesterday was National Random Act Of Kindness Day across Canada!"

The new tyre, the bike that worked again. The kindness, the awesomeness and the coincidence. I said goodbye to Heather, and rode with Mike as he guided the way to the border crossing. We soon reached the falls, which were now shrouded in damp fog, and we shook hands. In the daytime the Falls weren't lit up, they were just natural. I crossed over into the US for the final time, and sat at a park right on the lip of the falls with a view back across to the Canada side.

The roaring water, the unquantifiable amount that powerfully poured over the edge with every second. It was spectacular. Looking back across to Canada that day was quite a profound experience. The country had provided the highest highs and lowest lows. And I think, somewhere deep down, Canada had been an incubative environment of personal growth.

I looked across the water into the fog. The thought of the end continued to make me uneasy. This was life now.

36

Moving The World

POSTED TO VAGUEDIRECTION.COM ON NOVEMBER 8TH, 2013:

"I read an article months ago, straight after finishing the section of the journey from Florida to California. It was about someone called Jackie Loza's ride down the West Coast of the US. She was let go from her job and her trip was a way to figure out the next move. And because of that, it was more than a bike trip – it was a time that real decisions were made. Decisions that influenced where she is right now.

She said, "It reaffirmed that I could do anything I put my 100 percent effort into. When I got back, I felt like I could move the world."

You know when reading something plants it in your mind? I've thought about that article, about "moving the world" ever since.

Finishing the ride across the Southern Tier, I could totally relate to her thoughts. You get into trouble or have a bad day, you fix it. At the end of each day you know it's been a good day. That adds up, and over time, really makes you think that much bigger things are possible and that hurdles are made for crushing.

To end the trip there maybe would have been 'the sensible option'. It would have been a euphoric end, all highs. The cross country trip had been a success. Mountains would have been quivering at the thought of getting moved. Just kidding! But that stretch marked a small part of this overall journey. So reaching the Pacific, I thought – if you feel this bold / upbeat after three months, jeez, imagine what it will be like with more time.

But it's not a 45 degree graph where the good keeps rising. Good rose to 90 days and then the ruler stopped working and the rising line got bored and decided to go on a squiggle-spree. It hits the top of the page then the bottom, bottom then top. As the weeks and months go on, you go from empowerment / bring it on, to fuck this / I'm a loser, back to mountain moving / boulder lifting in this bizarre cycle of being confident and determined, to having no confidence at all and wanting to hide in a cave, back to being confident.

I could relate to Jackie using the trip as a vehicle to make big decisions. Over time, especially after a long day pedalling, your mind clears and you begin to slot pieces together. 'If I do X, then maybe Y will become a possibility'.

In those high 'move the world' moments, everything seems amazing, really like anything is possible. Like the cards on the table going forward shine more than they ever have before. Nothing is intimidating.

And then, on the down days, I've felt literally sick about time spent away, debt and potential irresponsibility, and whether there were opportunities left behind.

But so many of the people I've spoken to started by going all in and taking a shot, choosing a risk in the hope that opportunities down the line will bring more value than staying still.

I haven't got the faintest idea what happens next. It's kind of wide open. Some days that's a scary thing, and other days it's really invigorating, despite the questions that sometimes kick in.

But we all have doubts – whether what we're doing is what we should really be doing. That's natural. And those questions are good, because they make you think, and possibly change. The cliche's are true – journeys like this do open your eyes. In tough ways and in the best ways.

My head's all over the place at the moment, processing the end of a bizarre year. How squiggly can a graph get with five days left?

Today, the thought of finishing this thing is strangely nerve wracking, there's an anxiety there, certainly. Tomorrow might be completely different. It has a tendency to be."

37

Yeezy And A Poem

C ANADA USES KILOMETERS, AND THE UNITED STATES USE miles. Because of that, after crossing the Niagara River, time slowed down. It seemed to take an age for the distances to reduce on road signs, until remembering that I was back in New York State.

"Oh... Hold on... We've switched back to miles you idiot!"

Quick side note - talking to yourself out loud and in plural is perhaps a sign that a year is just the right amount of time before it's necessary to stop the journey, or check into a mental asylum.

Huge barns, churches and enormous houses flanked the flat roads, almost all displaying the stars-and-stripes flag, high and proudly. The conditions were just incredible. Every inch, set on a quiet backdrop of vividly coloured foliage which would've been at home on a Happy Autumn postcard.

The roads were mostly empty, so my headphones were set to loud – dangerously loud when the few cars passed by but dangerously fun when they didn't. And the order of the day was very loud hip-hop about getting popped by a cap and hangin' with hoes, still not togetherness and joy.

The rural turned to city suburbia, which soon turned to full on city downtown. This was Rochester, one of the first American boomtowns, known for it's flour mills. City planning had made the centre pedestrian-focused, with big sidewalks and parks.

A group of five people called over as I freewheeled down the sidewalk. Two women and three men in their late teens and early twenties. They were curious about the bike, until they saw my earbuds dangling, which shifted the conversation.

"What you listen to, man?" one of the guys asked. He was wearing a bright red hoody, and had proper full-size Beats By Dre headphones around his neck.

"A bunch of stuff really," I said like a rabbit in headlights, trying to think on the spot and being taken back in my mind to school days, where it was necessary to answer these type of questions in a cool way to avoid ridicule. "Lot's of hip-hop. The new Kanye and Jay Z album is pretty much on loop at the moment."

I love hip-hop music, which you might've gathered by this point, but if there was ever a time when I felt like a hip-hop fraud, now was it.

"Ahaha! Yeezy and Jigga? So lame, man."

We laughed. They suggested less "lame" music choices and laughed at my British accent.

"You know of Ricky Gervais, man? He's hilarious." It was always either James Bond, Prince Harry, or Ricky Gervais. Always.

Seneca Lake is one of The Finger Lakes - a pattern of lakes that are long and narrow, resembling fingers. They represent New York's Wine Country, and also some of the deepest lakes in the US. They've a reputation amongst fishing enthusiasts, and one of the towns in the area, Geneva, is known as the "Lake Trout Capital of the World."

Cycling down the edge of Seneca Lake, and losing track of the miles because of the views, I looked at the water and remembered fishing in Prince George with Les. A good day, a dark time. A time which seemed like so long ago, and reminded me yet again that this journey had been quite vast.

There was a huge, steep downhill. It was fast, all the way down to the infamous city of Ithaca.

Two friends, by coincidence, had sent messages with the same contents. Ithaka - a poem by Constantine P Cavafy. Maybe you come to the end of a long journey, and your emotions are all over the place, so you try to connect things and in doing so become a bit of a pansy, but this seemed quite powerful:

"When you set out for Ithaka
ask that your way be long,
full of adventure, full of instruction.
The Laistrygonians and the Cyclops,
angry Poseidon - do not fear them:
such as these you will never find
as long as your thought is lofty, as long as a rare
emotion touch your spirit and your body.
The Laistrygonians and the Cyclops,
angry Poseidon - you will not meet them
unless you carry them in your soul,
unless your soul raise them up before you.
Ask that your way be long.
At many a Summer dawn to enter
with what gratitude, what joy -
ports seen for the first time;
to stop at Phoenician trading centres,
and to buy good merchandise,
mother of pearl and coral, amber and ebony,
and sensuous perfumes of every kind,
sensuous perfumes as lavishly as you can;
to visit many Egyptian cities,
to gather stores of knowledge from the learned.
Have Ithaka always in your mind.
Your arrival there is what you are destined for.
But don't in the least hurry the journey.

> Better it last for years,
> so that when you reach the island you are old,
> rich with all you have gained on the way,
> not expecting Ithaka to give you wealth.
> Ithaka gave you a splendid journey.
> Without her you would not have set out.
> She hasn't anything else to give you.
> And if you find her poor, Ithaka hasn't deceived you.
> So wise you have become, of such experience,
> that already you'll have understood what these Ithakas mean."

After reading that I was all over the place, reduced to the emotional state of a baby who was hungry.

The value in this trip was not about a single moment, deep down I knew that. It was about the journey as a whole. I'd forgotten that many times, choosing to focus on frustrations, time limits and getting somewhere. Trying to find something else. Something in the future, rather than appreciating the now.

Ithaca was a rain-check. Life is not about specific moments, it's about everything.

38

Being And Peace

L IGHT SNOWFLAKES FELL ONTO THE DARK LEAVES EITHER side of the road. This was the absolute middle of nowhere. Being here had taken hours upon hours of cycling on ultra narrow, deserted, single lane farm roads. The air was fresh, the sun had long since gone down. There was no food in the panniers, all water was gone at this point.

You would've thought that if someone had spent a year on a bicycle they would've learned to not put themselves in these kind of situations time after time, wouldn't you?

I clicked the GPS on for the first time in months. The display lit up like a lantern in the night. Honesdale was 27.4 miles away. On these roads that was four, possibly five hours away. I set off, expecting to soon become demotivated and set up camp by the side of the road, starting the following day with a growling stomach and the shortest of tempers.

The Land Rover came from behind and drove past. Up ahead in the distance, it turned around and returned, like a circling shark. It stopped a few metres away, in the middle of the road, with it's blinding headlights on full beam making looking up impossible, which was a tad off-putting until I finally saw that the driver was a middle-aged blonde woman with a nice smile. Murderers don't have nice smiles.

"I couldn't just drive past," Marianna shouted from the driving seat. "You do know where you are, right?"

I explained about using the GPS to navigate to Honesdale.

"Are you mad?" She jumped in. "You won't get to Honesdale tonight, it's an hour to drive, let alone cycle. I live a mile away and have a beautiful cottage, right by the side of the lake. There's plenty of spare bedrooms, and my friend is staying with me tonight too, so there'll be three of us. Do you just want to stay and set off in the morning? Oh and we're having a steak dinner and have some lovely wine."

Let's break down what Marianna said. Beautiful cottage. Spare bedroom. Steak dinner. Lovely wine. Yes please.

"Well, I was kind of dreading the next few hours to be honest."

She wasn't kidding about the beautiful cottage. It was stunning, set on the shoreline of a silent Wrighter Lake. Lining the outside of the house, and tied above the waterline, were Buddhist prayer flags. Blue, white, red, green, yellow. Inside were intricately carved Buddha sculptures, the atmosphere intentionally calming, and the smell of incense far more pleasant than the more familiar one of unwashed socks.

Marianna shouted up the staircase and the friend she had mentioned, Elizabeth, in baggy trousers, walked downstairs.

The pair had been friends for a few years, after meeting at a Buddhist meditation retreat. Elizabeth had stopped by for a few days before driving cross country to start a new life in Santa Cruz, after a recent divorce.

In the lounge that overlooked the lake, lights from the other side flickered gently, causing reflections on the breeze-rippled water.

Elizabeth had recently been learning about astrology. Marianna adamantly insisted that the two of us should sit down with wine whilst she prepared the meal.

It was quite bizarre. Elizabeth needed to know certain things before she could apply her astrology skills on new people. She grabbed my hand tightly, and scanned the lines on my palm, nodding, absorbing and thinking. I hoped she wasn't a joker about to spit in my hand and say "in your future, there will be a swimming pool."

She asked about the exact time I was born. I had no idea what time of day I was born, but she pushed for an answer so I said 'maybe 11PM?', as though she was the midwife at the hospital that day and just wanted a reminder. But 11PM was all she needed, and we went from there.

She asked questions, and then looked at some cards and a website on her laptop.

Obviously the whole system is designed to provide one-size-fits-all insights, and is about as real as Hogwarts, but caught up in the calm environment, I was amazed at the accuracy. Everything Elizabeth spoke of was relatable in some way.

"You dream big, but are looking for something that's simple and can provide contentment and stability... You will have a major life change in the near-future... You will settle when the time is right..."

You get the idea. Totally airy fairy nonsense that everyone could apply to themselves. But at the time, I looked naively in disbelief, thinking, "Woah, that is crazy!" Maybe it was the wine.

Marianna called over and we gathered around the table. It was a standout meal. Steak, mushrooms, potatoes, onions, crunchy kale. A world away from the road diet. We ate and it was a happy time. A little whacky, too. Elizabeth brought out a small metal device, that she distractingly spun with her finger.

"It brings good energy into the room," she said, which was a little confusing. Maybe it was the wine.

Unaware of time passing, the conversation moved to the lounge again, and turned to the topic of Buddhism. It got quite deep, and it was clear that Marianna and Elizabeth were the real deal. Which was cool, because before that, in my experience, Buddhism had always been a bit of a 'trendy' thing, attracting students who liked the label and meditated only when someone was watching. Whereas these guys lived it, breathed it, and actually gave off good energy. A sentence about 'good energy' is something I never thought I'd write, by the way.

It was 4AM when we realised the time, and my mind was sore from trying to grasp some of the concepts about goals, contentment, mindfulness, and presence that Marianna and Elizabeth had tried to explain. "Just be," they'd say, over and over again, to simplify things for the dummy in the room.

In the morning, I walked outside, onto the pier overlooking the lake. This was peaceful. The only sounds around were the prayer flags quietly flapping in the wind, and the birds in the trees.

39

The Bridge,
The End

Monroe, New York. A place where, only once, on the last day, I fell over in a heap outside a funeral home.

As it got more and more built up, with every mile, New York City got closer.

Then the police officer turned on the flashing lights of his patrol car, and pulled over into the hard shoulder up ahead. He stepped out of the car and waited.

This was annoying, because I had just seen the city skyline on the horizon for the first time, and was in the zone, and was absolutely blasting down the road as though fate was nudging me forward. Wind was strong upon my back, which it rarely was, and Jay Z's Empire State Of Mind was intense upon my eardrums. It would be a blow to get arrested now.

"What on earth are you doing?" the officer got out of the car and screamed.

"Umm," I muttered, coming to a sudden stop, and not quite sure what the problem was, "what do you mean?"

The hard shoulder was wide and made a great cycle lane. It was much safer than many of the other roads I'd been spending time on.

"You're riding a bicycle on the highway!"

"Oh. Sorry. I thought this was okay."

Sometimes you can ride on highways legally, and when you can, they can be sensible roads to take. Sometimes you can't. Here you couldn't.

"I'm going to need you to give me your passport."

After handing it over, the policeman climbed inside his car to run background checks. "It's clean," he said, noticeably disappointed, "I need you to get off at the next exit, and to not ride on the highway outside America's biggest city ever again!"

Off the highway, the distance to George Washington Bridge was decreasing rapidly. The GPS was turned on again, indicating how many miles were left.

Less than ten miles.

Less than five.

Less than two.

Less than one.

There it was. The entrance to the bridge, just a small metal gate with a squeaky door. Now meters away, on the other side of the road.

'Not yet, it's not time.' Debilitating fear hit me, more than it ever had before.

It was scary to end. Scary to step back to normality. Scary to think about what came next. Even scary to see my folks who'd been amazing throughout, who'd provided a sounding board, and who were waiting on the bridge. I was scared they'd see a different person now, someone who'd been worn and who, face to face, they wouldn't recognise.

Next to the gate, I stepped off the bike and sat on a wall. 'What is wrong with you?' I thought.

It was freezing, but that was not the reason why I froze. My hands started to shake because of nerves, and a lump formed in my throat. It was very bizarre because I'm a tough and strong man who rarely shows emotion. Y'hear me?!

From an outside perceptive, this may seem ridiculous. This hadn't been a cutting-edge expedition, not a world first or a smashed record. So why, then, was going back on to that bridge such a frightening prospect?

These kind of trips are almost always done for personal reasons. People may claim that they're about culture, or exploration, or research, or fundraising, but in almost every case, that is a tiny part of the puzzle. The meat is in personal discovery. Testing yourself. Seeing what you're made of. Seeing how you'll cope. Developing over time. These journeys mean everything to those who embark on them.

The bike sat beside me, propped up against the wall. It had been my life for 368 days, the most valuable year I could remember. For that to suddenly cease was absolutely terrifying. I'd grown used to it.

I looked at the gate. At a distant time, this bridge had marked the beginning. That, like this, had been overwhelming and nerve-wracking, because I didn't know how it would work, or what was going to happen. Now, the coin seemed to have flipped.

I stood up. I clicked my shoes into the pedals for the last time, and began riding the bike, my home of uncomfortable comfort.

Through the gate.

A fast pulse.

Onto the smooth bridge.

The dark Hudson, majestic below.

The loop, closed.

Epilogue

TRAVEL STORIES OFTEN END WITH SOMEONE HEADING OFF into the sunset and living happily ever after. But I'm going to be honest - finishing the ride was a bit like getting hit in the face with a really big sledgehammer. It was a shock.

Reintegration was a real struggle. I'd heard that this might be an issue, but never really believed it. This wasn't returning from a war zone, after all. But feeling settled was far tougher than I'd thought it was going to be. Which is silly really - getting home after time away should be a really social period, spent making up for lost time and having lots of fun reconnecting. But that's not what happened at all, initially.

The vibrations of the motors, the rain on the windows, buzz of the TV's, jingles on the radio. Was this really the real world? I instantly missed the simplicity of the road.

Life felt difficult to hack, it wasn't a smooth re-entry at all. I was a complete fish out of water. A dry fish with anxiety issues. So instead of sticking around, I ran, just a few days after getting back. A job came up in Chile and being somewhere new felt more comfortable than being somewhere I knew. And getting back from that, nothing really changed, and for a while I constantly envisaged packing my bags.

I get worried sometimes, when the inclination to run away for a long time kicks in, which it still does now and then. Worried about having opened a can of worms. Worried that escapism may become a bit like a crack addiction, always tempting, and then thirty years will have gone past, and no life foundations will have been built.

It's good to do these things, to travel, to see things, to meet people, to build a wealth of experiences that you'll look back on forever. You could argue that it's absolutely vital, and I'd agree with you. It took time to realise, though, that at some point, maybe you ought to ask "why do I want to keep moving?'" and address that.

That's what I've been working on for the last year or so, to become less restless, to be more content with cherishing life and its everyday ups and downs. God knows I grew familiar with ups and downs on the ride itself. It hasn't always worked out, but I think, finally, I'm getting somewhere. Finally, I guess, that sunset scene is getting a little closer. The desire to run still exists, but it's a little faded, for now at least.

As I write this, it's April 2015. This book took longer to write than I ever imagined it would, and became more of a challenge than the ride ever was. The crispness of moments have begun diluting into distant memories, with each passing month. That's one of the most satisfying parts about writing this - some of those fading memories get to live on. And throughout, the process of writing it has been an immensely rewarding experience in and of itself. Cathartic in many ways.

In the midst of the day-to-day, I do regularly daydream back to moments on the road. And looking back now, it's possible to recognise the positive effects that this journey had. It had so many. I'll look back on it as a life highlight forever more.

Here's some takeaways that may apply to our broad life journeys:

Intimidation. It is in our mind. Obviously there's times when there's good reason to be hesitant and nervous, but so often those moments are fabricated within ourselves and, by avoiding what intimidates us, we miss out on worthwhile experiences.

The things that scare us are those we should face in order to grow.

Happiness shared. There's tons of value to be had from doing things solo and in isolation, but the truly happy memories come from shared experiences and connection.

Staying in the game. Grit beats skill. Determination and stubbornness beat knowledge. Keeping going is the easiest way to make something happen.

Roll with the punches. Shit goes wrong. It sucks but it's already happened and time machines aren't real yet. Reframe the negative into a learning experience, move on, and work it out – the process of working it out will probably be intrinsically worthwhile, and may lead to a hidden gain.

People are kind. Some may be standoffish, some may be scary, and some may be angry, but 99% of people have a warm side if you can build a connection with them. Regardless of who they are, what they do, or their outlook on life, there's a lot of value in connecting with new people.

Make your mission a moonshot. Setting moonshot goals, ones that seem scarily big, is a great way to learn quickly by default and surprise yourself. Dive in at the deep end, acknowledge that you don't know it all, and be okay with that. But try to remember that the climb might mean a lot more than the summit.

Time changes everything. I remember the rage, the occasional desperate desire to throw the bicycle off a bridge and never think about it again. But time will always alter an experience, and usually the tough times are the ones we eventually cherish. That's a beautiful part of human life.

Thank You

THIS TRIP, THIS BOOK, AND THIS ENTIRE PROJECT wouldn't have happened without a ton of really lovely people. Life's a collaboration, and the below are now well and truly legitimate members of Team Awesome. Ready? Go!

To the countless people who let this dirty traveller crash in their spare rooms or on their couches: Tracy and Alberta, Amie and Alberto, Sienna and Mariah, Shannon and Ryan, Jonathan and Karen, Heather and Mike, Steve Pope, Ned, Les and Barb, Emily and John, Theo, Shirley and Skip, Teresa, Blanch, Paresh, Jenn, Sophie, Bill at Winnipeg Guest House International.

To all of the people who were willing to be part of this journey in person:

HoYoung Jeong, Isaac and Sarah, Dora Sullivan, Jermaine Daniels, Meghan, Ned Brinkley, Alan Salmon, The Civil War Re-enactors, Misslette, Stefan Smith, Bert Miller, Ruben Fleischer, Samira Mostofi, Nick Thune, Mark Beaumont, Shannon Cecil, Sienna and Mariah Rowden, Matt Mullenweg, Guy Kawasaki, MC Hammer, Sophie Rubenstein, Katie Matten, Eileen Gittins, Martha Higareda, Bradford Haith, Michael Sulock, Busy, Wish, Martin and Jim, Tom Ethan, Joseph Wade, Joni and Valerie, Steve Pope, John Canfield, Adelaida Magallanes, Simon and Carol Bedford, Les and Barb Barna, Doug Riemer, Lawrence

Brennan, Connor Oliver-Beebe, Tim Koslo, Steve and Rachel, Sofia and Claudia, Teresa Roberts, Bill Macdonald, Mie Yaginuma, Andrew Sinkov, Martin Cheng, Erin Hall, Katie Johnson, Sierra Noble, Jolan Canrinus, Alistair and Jamie Nicholson, Gary and Wendy Foster.

I'm sorry if I've missed anyone, and I'm sorry too that many stories are missing from this book, but it would have to be a trilogy like Lord Of The Rings, and considering how long just this took to write, it would never get finished!

Special thanks to HoYoung - for being a friend and showing me the joy of mustard. To Jermaine - sorry! To Maria - for taking sides. To Ruben and Samira - for the uplift. To Brad - for sharing your story. To Sierra - for collaboration and laughter. To Misslette, Stefan and Bert - for letting me in to your world.

My ever-thanks to Evernote, the journeys title sponsor. They provide the best tools to remember everything. And to Magellan GPS, MET Helmets, The Body Rehab, Bergans, Goal Zero, Rode Microphones, Gemini Lights, Adventure Cycling, F-Stop Gear, Ghyllside Cycles, Marmot, Velocity Wheels.

To Graham Theobald - for keeping me going physically and motivationally. And to Mie Yaginuma - for taking the gamble, becoming a remote pillar of support, and for putting up with me!

To everyone who supported from afar when the journey looked bleak. It didn't fit as a theme in this book but it was a massive moment of encouragement and motivation. So an enormous thanks to all of you:

Mr and Mrs Gill Longway, Nigel Carruthers, Stuart and Brenda, Tomas Carlsson, George Foster, Jake Rogers, Paul and Susie Bate, Michael Hodges, Mike Cambray, Sulwen Roberts, Pete Otway, Paul Hampson, Rachel Treherne, George Ullrich, Mike and Marion, David Badcock, Robert Sloman, Roland Abbey, Nancy Cecil, Thomas Graham, Stuart Reid, Donald Pardoe, Kevin Brislin, Blaine Koch, Jack Bowhan, Graham Winder, Pat Batteson, David Bollom, Karen Brinklow, Rebecca Gledhill, Kat Bonney, May Kelly, Laura Cope, Andrew Woodhead, Gary Foster, Liam Lonsdale, Michael Ford, Jordan Roberts, Jeffrey McKinley, John Derbyshire, Tony Richardson,

Didier Richoux, Lynn Korol, Helen and John Matthews, Andy and Anne Rangecroft, Krysha Derbyshire.

To the really rad Kickstarter backers who helped take this story from a block of paper to what it is now:

Menno Dekhuyzen, Nancy Cecil, Paul Hampson, Barb Barna, Chris Stirling, Rob Dean, Rachel Wilson, Dan, Laura Valentine, Alistair Nicholson, Andrew Robb, Marie Corry, Diane Smillie, Bill Macdonald, Jay Howard, Jeremy Strutt, Chris Cook, Susie Bate, Phillipa Gladwin, Jeffrey Spence, Martyn Nicholson, Jim Cregan, Andy Sneesby, Geoff Broadway, Daniel Corning, Sienna Rowden, John Spooner, Kenneth Alexander, Mike Cambray, Eilidh Siegal, Steve Kloyda, Andy McKendry, Pete Otway, Jamie Nicholson, Eded Newell, Matthew Otway, Mark Cottam, Sam Dixon, Philip, Nicholas Hoepelman, Emma Jane Higgins, Lynx, Sam Smith, Jared Picune, El James, Nathan Dunn, Florian Theimer, Contessa Ricci, Dave Howard, Mark Pluijmakers, Robert T. Maisano, Janell Hoong, Kieran Brady, Rebecca Wright, Karen Brinklow, Arjen van Stijn, Tom Allen, Kevin Shannon, Jackie Couchman, Stuart Bell, Allysse Riordan, Lee Anderson, Mike Grenville, Liz Allen, Nathan Flash Savelli, Dawn Guest, Graham Jones, William Rodell, Mark Greenwood, Chris Fuller, Craig Allebach, Roger Mitchell, R Martin Seddon, Guy Huxtable, Jon Sykes, Michael Hodges, Dan Huse, Mike Thomas, Bill Neville, Lana Counce, Jeff Cover, Daniel Soh, Gregory Burger, David Gunlock, Carol Philip, Treena Kitchen, Liam, James Lander, Ben Robinson.

To the people who were involved in shaping and shipping this project, the designers, editors and creatives:

Hannah Cottrell for the branding.

Amanda Ashton for the typesetting.

Petra Blahova, Steve Scott, Jacqui Scott and Jenny Rice at Mountain Creative for the cover design.

John Mitchell for the copy editing and feedback.

Neil Gill for the application of his creative mind throughout.

To James and Neil - I will always look back on VC as an amazing chapter. Thank you, for the memories, the parties, the hustle, the shoots, the nights, the laughs, the naughtiness, the yoghurt drinks and the scotch eggs. Remember boys, we did it, we got to play with helicopters! Here's to a life full of moments.

To Neil and Kat - thank you for always being there, for your encouragement and for everything else. Could not've done this without your support. I can't wait for more fun when the Little One arrives.

Lastly, to my parents, Andy and Lesley. I am forever grateful for the support and generous encouragement you show to your unconventional child who might seem a bit slow to settle down. One day I will. Maybe. But honestly, this would not've happened without your support, so thank you from the bottom of my heart.

An Invitation

Wow, you made it, high five! There's tons of books out there, so it blows my mind that you read this one. Thank you!

Enjoyed it? Hated it? This is the first book I've written, so please let me know your thoughts by leaving a review on Amazon (www.vaguedirection.com/review will take you to the right place). Doing so would really help, and might possibly perhaps maybe definitely encourage me to write a few more.

Oh, and as a bonus, if you leave a review, email me with it and I'll reply with a treat. My email is dave@steepmedia.com. It'd be amazing to hear from anyone who took something away from this story.

And if you're reading this and are not yet a member of Team Awesome, then head to www.vaguedirection.com and subscribe. That's where I documented this journey as it happened, and that's where I'll continue to blog going forward. It'd be totally cracking to have you on the team.

Finally, please consider sharing this book around, and making it as tatty as possible by passing it on to anyone who may connect with it. Especially the daydreamers who need a push.

See you later, alligators.

Dave